Arts & Crafts for Home Decorating®

HALLOWEEN DECORATING

CREATIVE
PUBLISHING
international

Copyright © 1998 Creative Publishing international, Inc.
5900 Green Oak Drive Minnetonka, Minnesota 55343 • 1-800-328-3895 • All rights reserved • Printed in U.S.A.

Cataloging-in-Publication Data can be found on page 128

TABLE OF CONTENTS

Introduction 5

HALLOWEEN DECORATING

Halloween falls at the time of year when the last of the harvest is being gathered, the days are cooler, and the nights come earlier; mysteries of the dark form the basis of most tales and traditions. It's a time for children of all ages to enjoy the preparations as they invite witches and monsters and hobgoblins home.

Create a variety of projects to greet your visitors, from traditional pumpkin carving and child-friendly pumpkin painting to life-size figures and mats for the front door. Dispel the gloom of the night with luminaries and lighted swags.

Decorate your home with wreaths, swags, and tripods that showcase the harvest and Halloween tales. Create a bone-clattering skeleton, a spiderweb mobile, or a small haunted house. Quilt a scarecrow wall hanging. Prop fabric pumpkins or wooden shelf sitters next to whimsical picture frames or on a bewitching shelf.

Celebrate the season with a party. Create intriguing invitations from ordinary paper bags. Consider festive alternatives for a Halloween buffet. Decorate your table with runners, placemats, napkins, and coasters just right for the season. Make wired felt place cards and foam treat cups for your guests, and serve them Halloween goodies on painted glass. Set the stage with a haunting centerpiece, bathed in the eerie glow of spook-inspired candlelight.

OUTDOOR GREETINGS

PUMPKIN DECORATING

A carved jack-o'-lantern is the original Halloween luminary. Transforming pumpkins and squashes into glowing globes with friendly smiles or frightful sneers is the cornerstone activity for Halloween merrymaking. With the use of a few simple tools, elaborate expressions and spooky silhouettes are easily carved or sculpted by novice and artist alike. Inexpensive carving kits that include tiny saws, a poker for marking the pattern, and a miniature drill make pumpkin carving as easy as connecting the dots. Because of the sharp blades, carving and sculpting pumpkins requires careful adult participation, though older children can carve intricate designs

safely. Designs can also be sculpted into the surface of pumpkins and squashes using tools intended for other purposes: linoleum cutters cut fine lines; gouges and chisels cut deeper into the pulp.

Use the patterns on page 122, enlarging them as necessary. Or develop your own designs from simple line drawings. If you intend to carve, cutting completely through the pumpkin shell, be sure any area you want to silhouette will remain connected to the intact shell. Draw patterns for sculpting, shading areas as you want them to appear. Lighter areas are sculpted deeper, and

Greet Halloween night visitors *with a glowing array of carved and sculpted pumpkins and squashes. Or paint pumpkins with spirited designs, for lasting enjoyment during daylight hours.*

dark areas are left uncut. Incorporate both techniques into the same design, if you prefer.

Painted pumpkins can be used indoors as well as outside. Because the shells are uncut, they can be decorated long before Halloween and still look fresh for Thanksgiving. Painting on pumpkins is also a safer activity for younger children. Apply acrylic craft paints, using paintbrushes, foam applicators, or shapes cut from cellulose sponges.

Select firm pumpkins and squashes with sturdy stems, an indication that the pumpkins will last longer. Wash

them thoroughly with a weak bleach solution. Store the pumpkins at least 1" (2.5 cm) apart in a cool, dry, well-ventilated area. Do not allow them to freeze. Once cut, pumpkins may dry out and the edges will shrivel. For best results, carve or sculpt pumpkins less than 24 hours before use. Cover the opening and the design with plastic and keep them cold. If they will be displayed for an extended time, rub petroleum jelly on the exposed pulp.

Whether carving, sculpting, or painting a pumpkin, never set a pumpkin or candle directly on furniture. Never leave a candle unattended indoors. Place lit pumpkins where they won't tip or fall, and keep them out of the walkway.

MATERIALS

- Pumpkin or squash.
- Newspaper.
- Paper; pencil; scissors; tape.

For carving and sculpting:

- Small handsaw, 6" (15 cm) blade with narrow tip, for carving lid and large open areas.

- Ice cream scoop or sturdy spoon.
- Carving tools, such as awl, linoleum cutters, gouges, chisels, or melon ball tool.
- Candle and candle holder, size appropriate for pumpkin size.

For painting:

- Graphite paper.
- Acrylic paints.
- Artist's brushes; foam applicators; cellulose sponges.
- Permanent markers, optional.
- Aerosol clear acrylic sealer.

HOW TO CARVE A PUMPKIN

1 Cut an opening in the top or bottom of the pumpkin large enough for removing seeds and pulp. If cutting a top lid, angle tool inward, so lid will not fall into shell. If cutting bottom opening, cut straight into pumpkin. Cover work surface with newspaper. Clean out seeds and pulp, using ice cream scoop or spoon. Scrape shell wall to consistent 1" (2.5 cm) thickness.

2 Trace or draw a pattern on paper. Tape pattern to pumpkin; slash and lap pattern as necessary to fit pumpkin smoothly, without distorting design details. Poke small holes every 1/8" (3 mm) along all design lines, using pushpin, awl, or poking tool. Remove pattern; set aside. Connect dots in intricate areas with pencil.

4 Carve small details first, working from center of design outward. Hold saw perpendicular to surface; saw gently, dot to dot. Remove and reinsert blade to turn corners. Keep free hand away from saw; avoid pressing on carved areas. Saw large pieces into smaller pieces; push them out with your fingers. Trim excess pulp around the openings, cutting at slight angle.

3 Gently twist small drill or drill bit to cut any round holes, keeping drill perpendicular to the pumpkin surface. For tiny points of light, push awl or poking tool entirely through the pumpkin shell.

HOW TO SCULPT A PUMPKIN OR SQUASH

1 Follow steps 1 and 2, opposite. Carve simple lines first, using linoleum cutter, gouge, or chisel. Rotate pumpkin, always cutting away from body; stabilize pumpkin from behind cutting tool, to avoid cutting hand.

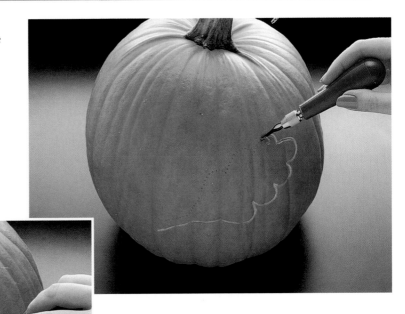

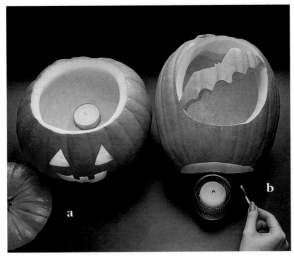

2 Sculpt light and medium areas of design, cutting away desired amount of pulp. The deeper the cuts, the more light will shine through. To sculpt large area, cut away pulp, using melon ball tool.

HOW TO LIGHT A CARVED OR SCULPTED PUMPKIN

1 For pumpkin with lid **(a),** scoop hole ½" (1.3 cm) deep in shell floor; secure candle. Light candle; replace lid. For bottom opening **(b),** set candle in small candleholder; set pumpkin over burning candle. Allow to burn for a few minutes.

2 Punch small hole through shell ceiling or lid, marking area darkened by candle. From outside, cut 1" (2.5 cm) vent hole around the mark.

OUTDOOR GREETINGS

11

Transfer intricate designs, using graphite paper. Draw simple designs freehand, using pencil or felt-tip pen.

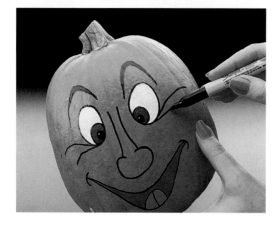

Add bold design lines, using permanent markers.

Apply acrylic paint, using artist's brushes or small foam applicators. Paint background colors first. Allow the paint to dry thoroughly before applying foreground colors. Apply two or three coats as necessary.

MORE IDEAS FOR DECORATING

Incorporate odd shapes or blemishes into your design, rather than hide them. Lay pumpkin on its side and use the stem for a nose. Change bumps and nodes into warts or beauty marks.

Spray dry designs with
aerosol clear acrylic sealer.

Cut Halloween shapes from
cellulose sponges (below).
Coat surface of sponge with
paint; roll across pumpkin
surface for even coverage.

PUMPKINS
& SQUASHES

*Stack carved or painted
pumpkins or squashes to
create Halloween creatures.
Join them with sturdy tooth-
picks or wood skewers.*

GHOSTLY TRICK-OR-TREATER

Surprise trick-or-treaters who come knocking at your door with this little guy to greet them. He looks so real that you may even try to load his trick-or-treat basket when you're filling all the others!

Under his felt ghost costume is a simple support system of wooden dowels, wire, and Styrofoam® balls. Use jeans and shoes that a child has outgrown for a touch of reality; shop at a local thrift store if you don't have anything close at hand. Top off the little character with a child's baseball cap. Then sit back and listen to others say hello to him before they ring your doorbell. When you trick them, you have to treat them, too!

HOW TO MAKE A GHOSTLY TRICK-OR-TREATER

MATERIALS

- 18-gauge wire; wire cutter.
- Two Styrofoam balls; 1" (2.5 cm), for nose; 6" (15 cm), for head.
- Two ⅜" (1 cm) dowels, 36" (91.5 cm) long.
- One pair used children's shoes, size 7 to 9½.
- Two plastic bags to fit inside shoes.
- Plaster of Paris and disposable container for mixing.
- One pair used children's jeans, size 3 to 5.
- Newspaper.

- Hot glue gun.
- 1¾ yd. (1.6 m) white felt, 72" (183 cm) wide.
- Straightedge; pencil; scissors.
- Black fabric scrap, for eyes.
- Paper-backed fusible web and iron.
- Purchased trick-or-treat basket.
- Child's cap.

1 Cut 6" (15 cm) length of wire; fold into tight "U" shape. Poke ends through small Styrofoam ball and into large Styrofoam ball, for head.

2 Line shoes with plastic bags. Prepare plaster of Paris, following manufacturer's directions. Pour plaster into bags, filling shoes. Set aside to harden; insert dowels into shoes and prop upright just before plaster is fully set. Allow to dry thoroughly.

(Continued)

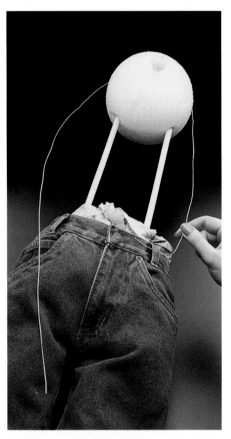

3 Tuck plastic bags into shoes. Slip jeans legs over dowels; stuff jeans with newspaper for body shape. Push both dowels into head so nose is positioned properly; secure with hot glue. Push wire through head, from side to side; secure one end to jeans belt loop.

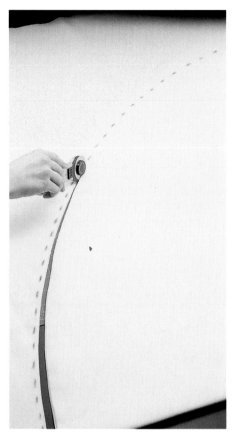

4 Fold felt in half lengthwise, then crosswise. Using straight-edge and pencil, mark an arc on felt, 30" (76 cm) from folded center. Cut on the marked line through all layers. Drape unfolded felt over head so lower edge is even.

5 Draw two ovals on paper side of fusible web. Bond to black fabric, following manufacturer's directions. Cut out ovals; pin to felt at eye level. Remove felt; fuse ovals in place.

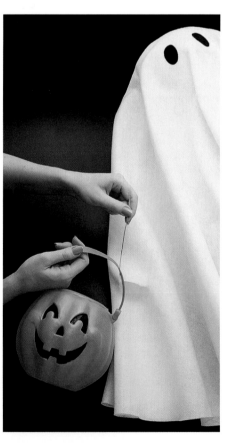

6 Replace felt over head. Cut 3" (7.5 cm) horizontal slit in felt, at hip level, on side where wire is unsecured. Bring wire through slit; wrap around purchased trick-or-treat basket.

WELCOME WITCH

Beware of Esmerelda. Flying just above the ground, she greets your Halloween visitors. Place her along the walkway or near the front door. You can create other welcoming figures, drawing your own patterns or enlarging and tracing favorite Halloween shapes.

Purchase an exterior plywood with a weather-resistant glue because regular plywood may split and warp when wet, even if it is painted and sealed; find 1/4" (6 mm) exterior plywood at wood hobby stores or 3/8" (1 cm) at lumberyards. Buy regular plywood if you plan to stand her on your porch or even inside.

Make simple stakes from two clothes hangers and push them easily into the ground to keep Esmerelda from falling in mid-flight.

MATERIALS

- ¼" or ⅜" (6 mm or 1 cm) plywood, about 12" × 24" (30.5 × 61 cm).
- Graphite paper.
- Masking tape.
- Coping saw or jigsaw.
- Medium-grit sandpaper.

- ⅜" (1 cm) dowel, 36" (91.5 cm) long.
- Wood glue.
- 9½" × 9½" × ¾" (24.3 × 24.3 × 2 cm) board, for base.
- Drill; 1/16", ⅛", and ⅜" drill bits.
- 28-gauge wire and wire cutter.

- Sanding sealer.
- Acrylic paint, colors as desired.
- Polyurethane.
- Two wire clothes hangers.

1 Enlarge the pattern (page 124); cut out. Trace onto plywood. Cut along marked lines, using saw. Sand rough edges.

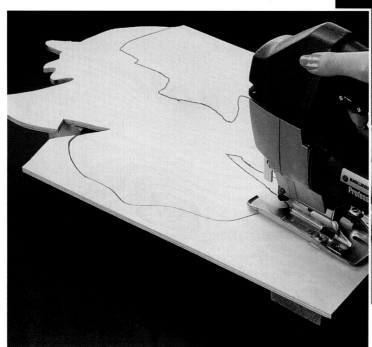

2 Mark dowel 2" (5 cm) from one end. Round end slightly; flatten one side above mark, using sandpaper.

3 Glue flat side of dowel to back of cut shape. Drill two holes on each side of dowel, using 1/16" drill bit; space holes ¼" (6 mm) apart. Pass wire through each hole two or three times, pulling snug. Twist ends together; trim ends.

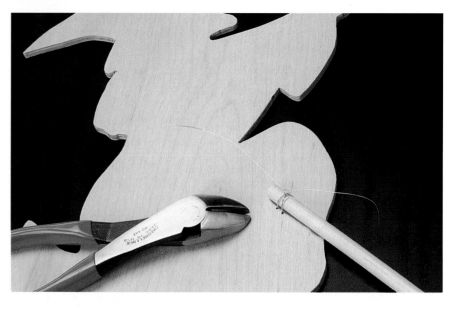

4 Wrap tape around ⅜" drill bit with edge of tape ⅝" (1.5 cm) from tip. Drill hole at center of base, stopping when edge of tape meets surface of wood. To stake base in lawn, drill hole through base, ¾" (2 cm) from each side center, using ⅛" drill bit. Sand rough edges. Glue dowel in center hole of board.

5 Apply sanding sealer to witch, dowel, and base. Paint as desired; allow to dry. Apply polyurethane; allow to dry. Form two stakes from each hanger, if desired. Cut wire 5" (12.5 cm) from each lower corner, bend wire 1" (2.5 cm) beyond corners, and trim second side to 5" (12.5 cm). Insert stakes through base holes and into ground.

SCARECROW

Stand this proud scarecrow to guard your home and greet your friendly visitors. Dress him in cast-off clothing and stuff him with raffia. Collect pumpkins and hay bales at his feet and set a raven on his shoulder to show the world that he, too, is a friendly guy.

Find suitable clothing as close as a child's closet or find something inexpensive at a local thrift shop. Look for pants that have a snap inseam for convenience, or cut a small hole just behind the crotch seams. Select from a wide variety of hat styles and embellishments to make your scarecrow unique.

HOW TO MAKE A SCARECROW

MATERIALS

- 9½" × 9½" × ¾" (24.3 × 24.3 × 2 cm) board, for base.
- Saw; sandpaper.
- Drill; ½" and 3⁄32" drill bits.
- ½" × 36" (1.3 × 91.5 cm) wood dowel.
- Wood glue.
- Sealer, such as water-based polyurethane.
- Paint or stain, for stand.

- #212 screw eye.
- Child's bib overalls, size 4, or jeans and four large safety pins.
- 24-oz. (750 g) packages raffia.
- 18-gauge wire.
- Plastic hanger.
- Child's flannel shirt, size 4, used.
- Scissors.
- 5⁄8 yd. (0.6 m) burlap.

- Hot glue gun.
- 6" (15 cm) Styrofoam® ball.
- Twine.
- Paints, for face.
- Hat.
- Embellishments as desired; raven; bandanna; fall flowers or miniature corncobs.

1 Drill hole through base center, using ½" drill bit. Sand rough edges. Glue dowel into base; allow to dry. Paint or stain as desired; dry. Apply two coats of sealer, following manufacturer's directions. Predrill hole for screw eye on front of dowel, 2" (5 cm) from top, using 3⁄32" drill bit; insert screw eye. Drop overalls or jeans onto dowel through inseam crotch.

2 Cut 9" (23 cm) length of 18-gauge wire. Form 8 oz. (250 g) raffia into bundle. Wrap wire around center; pull tight, and twist wires once or twice, leaving excess length.

(Continued)

3 Wire hanger, upside down, to back of dowel at screw eye. Wire raffia bundle to hanger hook; wire hook to dowel, using excess wire of raffia bundle. Reach into each leg and pull raffia through; allow raffia to puddle on base.

4 Repeat step 2 to make second raffia bundle; separate wire tails. Assemble third raffia bundle; lay over second bundle. Wrap and twist wires to secure.

5 Wire double raffia bundle to front of dowel at screw eye; separate bundles. Wire third raffia bundle loosely to hanger ends.

6 Slip the shirt over hanger. Reach through unbuttoned sleeves and pull third bundle out. Scrunch sleeves or roll cuffs so sleeve ends are about 24" (61 cm) apart.

7 Button shirt, and tuck into pants with second bundle. Add more raffia to fatten waist area, if desired. Hook shoulder straps to bib, or pin shirt inside jeans. Trim raffia at hands to about 3" (7.5 cm). Trim feet, if desired.

8 Push Styrofoam® ball onto dowel end until it hits the screw eye. Remove ball. Apply glue to hole and dowel; reposition ball on dowel, for head.

10 Center burlap over head; lap at back, and tie at neck with twine or raffia. Ravel burlap, if desired. Add facial details, using acrylic paints. Tie bandanna around neck, hiding twine, if desired. Add other embellishments as desired.

9 Fold the burlap in half lengthwise, then cross-wise; pin. Mark an arc on burlap, measuring 11" (28 cm) from folded center. Cut on marked line through all layers. Trim away one quarter of the circle.

LUMINARIES

Help visiting spirits find their way to your door by placing these luminaries along your walkway, steps, or porch. Or use them to lighten the spookiest, darkest recesses of your yard. Paint the luminaries with bright colors if visitors are expected early; watch the decorations transform into eerie specters as the sun goes down and the bats come out.

Use large tin cans with a diameter of at least 4" (10 cm). Purchase paint cans with handles and rounded edges at paint stores. Or collect and recycle coffee cans, tall juice cans, and large fruit and vegetable cans. Paint the can's outside black to eliminate unwanted reflections, and paint the inside white or yellow to improve its eerie glow. Pour sand in the bottom to weight the can and to provide a secure candle holder.

Fill the cans with water and freeze them. The ice supports the sides of the can as you punch the holes. You may want to use gloves to protect your hands from cold and from the sharp edges of the can.

For best results, purchase inexpensive punching tools, such as awls with sharp points and engravers with sharp, wide ends, at craft stores. Or substitute nails, small sharpened screwdrivers, and chisels.

HOW TO MAKE A LUMINARY

MATERIALS

- Cans, assorted sizes as desired.
- Permanent marker; paper; tape.
- Large towel; gloves, optional.
- Punching tools, such as engraver, small sharpened screwdriver, chisel, awl, and nails.
- Hammer.
- Spray paint in desired colors.
- Sand.
- Candle; long wooden matches.

1 Fill can with water; freeze solid. Copy or enlarge a linear design appropriate for the can size; mark locations of small and large holes, and short dashes. Tape pattern to can, away from any seams.

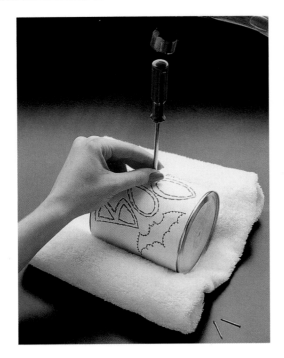

2 Fold the towel in half lengthwise; place on work surface and roll ends in toward can. Hold the punching tool at right angle to surface, resting the point on pattern. Strike with hammer, driving point through pattern and can surface. Complete entire design; remove pattern. Allow ice to melt.

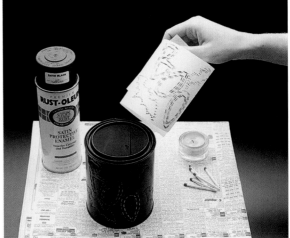

3 Spray can interior white or yellow, if it is dark; allow to dry. Spray exterior, if desired; line can with paper to catch overspray. Remove paper. Pour sand into bottom of can. Push candle into sand; avoid touching sharp edges on inside of can. Place luminary outside, and light candle.

LIGHTED SWAG

Colorful images allow visitors to enjoy this swag before the sun goes down, but it's even more fun in the dark! Children of all ages will enjoy making the simple decorations that appear in the black night behind small lights.

Purchase lightweight foam sheets, available in many colors, at craft stores, and cut delightful or frightful shapes, using ordinary scissors. Use cookie cutters for inspiration, or develop your own designs, incorporating a miniature light bulb. Try a jack-o'-lantern with an extra-bright nose or a fire-breathing dragon.

Avoid dark foam colors for the primary shape, since they will melt into the blackness beyond; reserve dark colors for surface embellishments. Just in case the weather turns wet and gloomy, secure design layers with a low-temperature glue gun or a waterproof glue.

HOW TO MAKE A LIGHTED SWAG

MATERIALS

- Foam sheets, assorted colors.
- Cookie cutters, optional.
- Pencil.
- Scissors with plain or decorative-edge blades.
- Low-temperature glue gun or waterproof glue.
- Mat knife.
- Permanent markers, optional.
- Weatherproof miniature lights.
- Grapevine or honeysuckle swag.

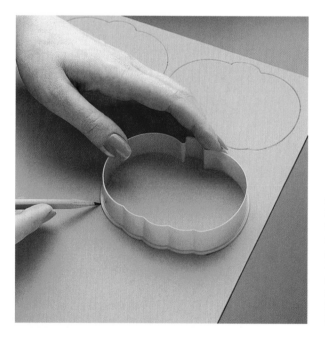

1 Cut simple Halloween shapes from craft foam, using cookie cutters for patterns or drawing designs as desired. Cut two ¼" (6 mm) crossed slits in each shape at desired location for light, using mat knife.

2 Embellish shapes as desired; attach foam detail shapes, using glue for added dimension, or draw design lines, using markers.

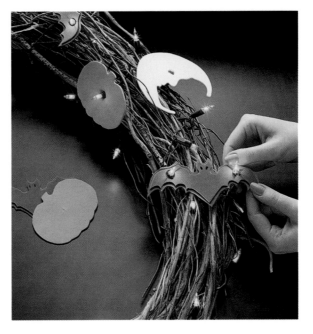

3 Entwine string of lights throughout swag, spacing lights evenly and pointing lights toward front of swag. Push crossed slits over the light and bulb housing. Pull foam back to edge of housing and bulb, turning slit edges back.

DOOR MATS

Fast and easy door mats, made from half-moon Kreative Kanvas® rugs, are a perfect project for kids. Make the threshold mat more visible from the walkway by securing a second mat to the door, using double-stick tape; create a design that seems to crawl up the door or one that emphasizes a round shape.

Tape curling rug edges to a hard work surface, or flatten the rug, using a cool iron; avoid high temperatures because of the rug's plastic core. Give young artists a box of crayons or markers and let their imaginations fly. Or provide acrylic or latex paints for an easy soap-and-water cleanup alternative. Draw designs freehand, using pencil lightly, or trace around cut-out patterns, if desired; the rug withstands gentle erasing. Trim the mat's outer edges, using regular scissors or a decorative-edge rotary cutter, if you want to accentuate a design; avoid long, narrow extensions, which won't withstand scuffing.

Seal the mat for durability and easy cleaning. Choose a water-based polyurethane or nonyellowing varnish for mats colored with crayons, permanent markers, or paint; choose oil-based sealers for rugs colored with washable markers.

HOW TO MAKE A DOOR MAT

MATERIALS

- Half-moon Kreative Kanvas rug, 18" × 36" (46 × 91.5 cm).

- Paper; tape; pencil.

- Scissors with plain or decorative-edge blades, mat knife and cutting surface, optional.

- Markers, assorted colors, optional.

- Crayons, paper towel or newsprint, iron, optional.

- Acrylic or latex paints, newspaper, brushes, optional.

- Sealer, such as polyurethane or nonyellowing varnish.

- Synthetic-bristle paintbrush, for applying sealer.

- Double-stick tape, optional.

1 Draw design on rug freehand, using pencil lightly, or enlarge motifs on photocopier to desired size and trace around cut-out shapes.

2 Color light areas first; fill in an area, if using crayons, or slightly cover lines, if using markers or painting. Allow paint to dry before applying adjacent colors.

3 Place paper towel or newsprint over crayon designs and press with cool iron. Apply sealer, using synthetic-bristle paintbrush; allow to dry several hours. Apply two more coats of sealer, following manufacturer's directions for drying time. Apply sealer to wrong side of mat.

STENCILED RUGS

This easy and inexpensive stenciled rug, made from a carpet sample, greets your Halloween visitors. An easy shake will clean it, and it stands up to a vacuum or a damp sponge, too.

Choose a carpet sample with a short, dense pile. Enlarge designs from other projects or create your own. Keep designs simple; the texture of the carpet is too coarse for fine details.

Cut a stencil of self-adhesive vinyl. Draw designs free-hand, or trace a design using graphite paper or by holding it up to a light source. The stencil must adhere

well to the carpet; press firmly around the cut edges of the stencil to improve the bond.

Condition the paint with fabric medium, following the manufacturer's directions, or thin two parts paint with one part water so the paint will be absorbed into the pile. Apply paint in an up-and-down motion rather than a sweeping motion to get a thorough coat and avoid paint seepage under the cut edges of the stencil. For durability, heat-set the paint with a hair dryer. When completed, seal the surface with clear acrylic sealer, if desired.

HOW TO MAKE A STENCILED RUG

MATERIALS

- Carpet sample with bound edges.
- Self-adhesive vinyl, such as Con-Tact®.
- Graphite paper, optional.
- Mat knife and cutting surface.
- Acrylic paints.
- Fabric medium, optional.
- Firm stencil brush or sponge applicator.
- Hair dryer.
- Stiff brush.
- Aerosol clear acrylic sealer, optional.

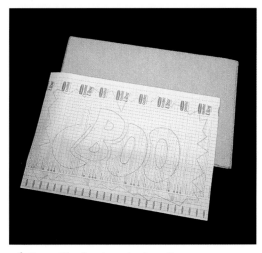

1 Cut self-adhesive vinyl to fit carpet sample. Draw or trace design, including outer border, on paper side of vinyl; draw mirror image of any letters or numbers.

2 Cut away areas to be stenciled, using mat knife or scissors. Remove paper backing from stencil carefully; press firmly onto carpet.

4 Remove stencil. Apply additional stencils, if desired. Allow to dry. Heat-set paint with hair dryer. Use stiff brush to soften painted areas. Apply sealer, if desired.

3 Apply conditioned or thinned paint to exposed carpet, using stencil brush or sponge applicator. Use an up-and-down motion, working paint into the fibers. Allow to dry.

HARVEST WREATH

This beautiful grapevine wreath is the perfect accent for a wall or door as it brings the colors of the season inside. By removing the Halloween cookie cutters, you can extend the life of the wreath into the Thanksgiving harvest season.

Secure larger items to the wreath with floral wire; secure smaller items with hot glue. Flexible wire, available on a paddle, is cut to the desired length; stem wire is stiffer and is packaged in 18" (46 cm) lengths. When covered with brown floral tape, wires blend with the smaller branches of the grapevine. The use of floral spray paints is optional; they may be used to deepen natural tones, to introduce gold highlights, or to provide a rich sheen.

HOW TO MAKE A HARVEST WREATH

MATERIALS

- 18" (46 cm) grapevine wreath.
- Floral wire, wire cutter; wired wooden floral picks; brown floral tape.
- Indian corn ears with husks, assorted sizes.
- Pinecones; acorns, assorted sizes.
- Miniature pumpkins, fresh or artificial.
- Lotus pods.
- Copper Halloween cookie cutters.
- Hot glue gun.

1 Wrap taped floral wire around corn, between ears and husk; secure corn to wreath, twisting wire ends.

2 Wrap wire around bottom layers of larger pinecones, twisting to secure. Use wire or glue to attach group of medium and large cones near each ear of corn. Push wire through fresh pumpkins or push wired pick into artificial pumpkins. Wrap wire around wreath near lowest ear of corn; twist to secure.

(Continued)

3 Glue lotus pods behind cones; add husks as desired. Use small cones and acorns to hide corn wires and enhance groups of pods and cones.

4 Attach cookie cutters to floral picks; wire to wreath behind pinecones. Twist taped wire to form loop; wrap ends around top of wreath for hanger.

MORE WREATH IDEAS

Substitute wired felt forms (page 102) or painted cardboard shapes for the cookie cutters.

Black-tie skeleton
(page 49) nestles
comfortably in the
curve of the wreath.
Secure the skeleton,
using fine wire or
monofilament line.

*Substitute colorful fall
leaves* for the locust pods
and cones. Replace the
Indian corn with fall
florals, such as mums or
sunflowers.

HALLOWEEN SWAG

B Birds, bats, and spiders find an inviting perch in this eerie Halloween swag. The wild, mysterious look of this piece is achieved in the selection of its elements. Look for dried naturals in dark, rich colors, and complement them with lighter tones. Artemisia, for example, is a silvery green, though you may also find it dyed other colors. Curly ting-ting is a thin, spiraling branch available in a variety of colors. Black Beard wheat offers a dramatic accent, both in shape and color.

Use fresh gourds and pumpkins if you intend to keep the swag for only a short time. Once they are pierced with wire, they will begin to disintegrate. Substitute dried or artificial items to extend the life of the swag.

HOW TO MAKE A HALLOWEEN SWAG

MATERIALS

- Twigs, honeysuckle vine, and grapevine pieces, 36" to 40" (91.5 to 102 cm) long.
- Floral wire; wire cutter; brown floral tape.
- Floral foam for dried arranging; serrated knife.
- Gray moss.
- Hot glue gun.
- Dried naturals, including artemisia, Sweet Annie, Black Beard wheat, step grass, and curly ting-ting.
- Small gourds; miniature pumpkins.

- Floral picks, drill and small drill bit, optional.
- Miniature ears red popcorn.
- Antique gold wax-based paint, optional.
- Old nylon hose, gray; scissors.
- Plastic spiders; heavy invisible thread.
- Blackbird, 2" to 3" (5 to 7.5 cm) long, on pick.
- Wired felt bats (page 102) or plastic clip-on bats.

1 Form swag with twigs, honeysuckle vine, and grape-vine pieces; bind with taped wire about one-third of the distance from each end. Twist taped wire to form loop for hanging; secure one loop behind each binding wire.

2 Cut five foam pieces ½" (1.3 cm) thick, and glue to central length of swag. Glue moss to swag, covering the foam.

3 Apply glue to ends of dried naturals; insert into foam from left and right of center. Add curly ting-ting.

(Continued)

4 Rub gold wax-based paint onto gourds or pumpkins, if desired. Push wire through fresh gourds. Insert wire ends through foam and around several vine pieces; twist ends, and trim. Or insert a pick well into drilled hole of dried gourd. Apply glue to both ends of pick and insert into foam as vertically as possible.

5 Shred gray nylon hose with scissors and fingernails. Drape, twist, and stretch hose over and around vines and moss to imitate cobwebs.

6 Rub gold wax-based paint onto corn ear kernels and husks as desired. Wrap taped wire around corn, between ears and husks. Secure corn to swag.

7 Glue spiders to the cobweb; use invisible thread to dangle the spiders, if desired. Push blackbird into the foam. Attach bats to ting-ting.

TRIPOD CENTERPIECE

T his haunting arrangement seems to have come from the distant corner of a crumbling mansion. Long forgotten, the crows and spiders have made it their home, and even a couple of bats find it welcoming.

The tripod consists of three sturdy branches about 25" (63.5 cm) long and about ½" (1.3 cm) in diameter at their thickest. Look for branches with interesting twists and nubby knots. Three similar sticks are used to brace the tripod form.

A small handleless basket or bird's nest holds the fall harvest. Fresh gourds and pumpkins may be used for a week or two, but select dried or artificial varieties if you plan to keep the arrangement for a long time. The eerie cobwebs are actually shredded nylon hose!

HOW TO MAKE A TRIPOD CENTERPIECE

MATERIALS

- Three branches and three small sticks.
- Floral wire; wire cutter; brown floral tape.
- Shallow basket or bird's nest, 5" to 6" (12.5 to 15 cm) in diameter.
- Small weights, optional.
- Floral foam for dried arranging; serrated knife.
- Green moss.
- Floral pins.
- Small gourds or miniature pumpkins.
- Gold wax-based paint, optional.
- Floral picks, drill and small drill bit, optional.
- Pods.
- Black crow, about 4" (10 cm) long.
- Old nylon hose, gray; scissors.
- Small plastic spiders.
- Wired felt bats (page 102).
- Hot glue gun.

1 Wrap branches together about mid-length, using taped wire. Spread thicker ends to form tripod. Attach basket rim to each branch with taped wire; twist and trim excess wire length.

2 Brace tripod with three small sticks; wire to branches just below the basket. Glue small weights inside basket to stabilize, if desired.

3 Cut foam, using knife, so it fits basket snugly and sits ½" (1.3 cm) below rim. Glue foam into basket. Secure moss over foam with floral pins. Glue moss pieces over each wired joint.

4 Rub gold wax-based paint onto two or three gourds, if desired. Attach all gourds and pumpkins to basket, using wire, floral picks, or hot glue. Push pods into foam near outer edge of basket.

5 Shred two or three pieces of nylon hose, using scissors or fingernails. Drape, twist, and stretch hose over branches to resemble cobwebs.

6 Glue crow to moss at upper joint. Glue spiders to cobwebs; attach bats to top branches.

Substitute a plastic witch's cauldron *for the tripod basket. Use small straw brooms, reinforced with dowels, for the three legs of the tripod; bind them with raffia or twine. Build a fire of small branches below the cauldron, with red foil to imitate the flames. Attach a glittering moon to an upper limb and a giant bat or raven to guard the brew.*

Substitute a carved pumpkin or a foam jack-o'-lantern for the basket. Perch a beanbag pumpkin (page 71) overhead and arrange little wired felt ghosts to dance among the branches.

Cut the top from a Styrofoam® pumpkin, using a serrated knife. Paint the inside and rim to match the outside.

Add miniature brooms to the swag. Wind a string of lights covered with witch and moon foam shapes through the swag. Substitute leaves for gourds. Wire the swag to a straight branch for support.

BEWITCHING SHELF

This beguiling witch with her haunting smile will be a whimsical addition to any room. There's a touch of good witchcraft about her—the hat brim is also a shelf. It's the perfect place for an extra candle, a friendly gourd, or a favorite black cat. When this shelf hangs on the wall, it's easy to see who's the fairest of them all!

HOW TO MAKE A WITCH SHELF

MATERIALS

- ¼" (6 mm) finish-grade plywood, for face.
- ½" × 6" (1.3 × 15 cm) poplar board, at least 18" (46 cm) long, for hat brim.
- Graphite paper.
- Jigsaw; clamp.
- Drill; ⅛" combination drill and countersink bit.
- Wood glue.
- Four #8 × 1⅝" (4 cm) coarse-thread drywall screws.
- 180-grit sandpaper.
- Acrylic paints in desired colors.
- Two sawtooth hangers.

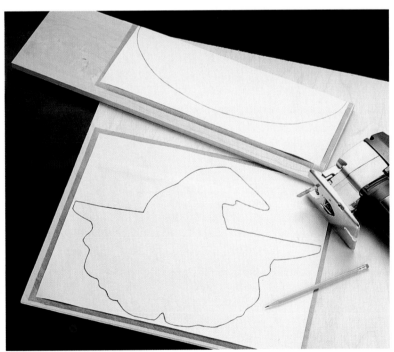

1 Enlarge witch's face pattern (page 125). Draw pattern for brim shelf 5" (12.5 cm) deep at center, with length equal to enlarged pattern brim; curve front brim edge toward sides. Tape patterns over graphite paper on wood; trace outlines and design lines. Cut out, using jigsaw.

(Continued)

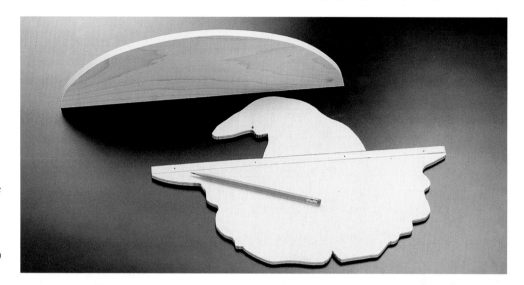

2 Stand the brim back on wrong side of face; align brim's upper side with face's straight edge. Mark each side of brim; set brim aside. Mark placement for four evenly spaced pilot holes halfway between brim lines; mark outer holes about 1" (2.5 cm) from ends.

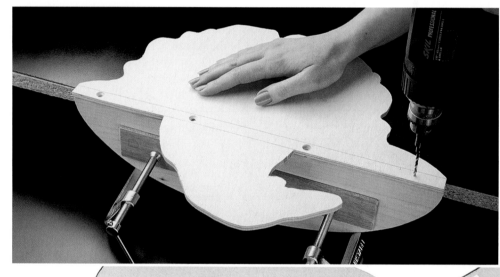

3 Secure brim in clamp so straight edge is at top. Place right side of face on brim; align straight edge with brim top. Drill holes with countersink bit at each mark.

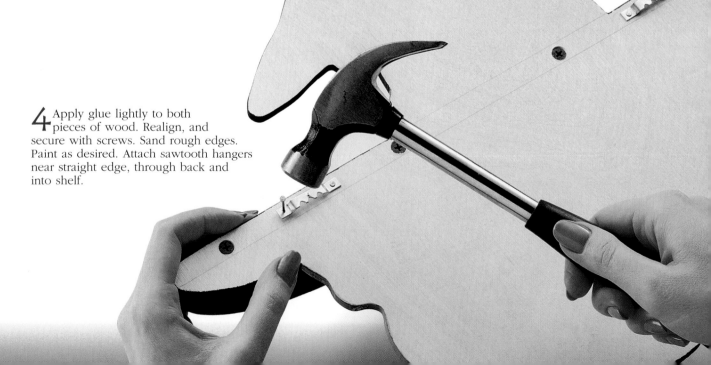

4 Apply glue lightly to both pieces of wood. Realign, and secure with screws. Sand rough edges. Paint as desired. Attach sawtooth hangers near straight edge, through back and into shelf.

BLACK-TIE SKELETON

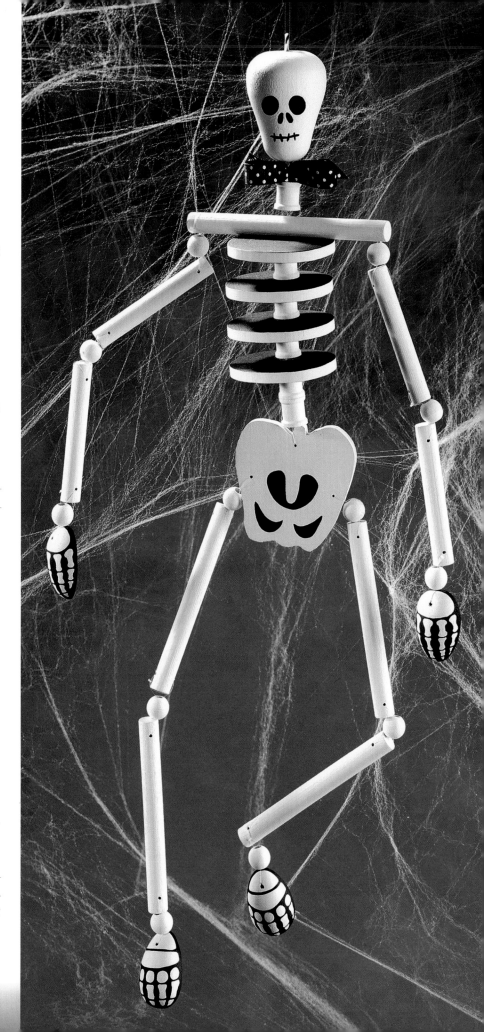

H Haunt your house with the eerie sound of dry bones clickety-clacking in the wind. Hang this black-tie skeleton on your front door where it will clatter every time you greet a friendly monster. Pose him reclining in the curve of a wreath or seated, with legs dangling from a shelf.

Aside from his dowel limbs, all of his parts are made from precut wood pieces and beads, available at craft and hobby stores. Paint Mr. Bones with acrylic paints, following the example here, or leave him unpainted for a natural look.

MATERIALS

- ⅜" (1 cm) wood dowel, 36" (91.5 cm) long.
- Wood pear, 2" (5 cm) high.
- One wooden apple cutout, 2¼" (6 cm) high.
- Four 2" × 1⅝" (5 × 4 cm) oval wooden cutouts.
- Six ½" × ½" (1.3 × 1.3 cm) wooden spools.
- Four small wooden split robin eggs.
- Twelve 10 mm round wooden beads.
- Two screw eyes, size #214.
- Small saw; 100-grit sandpaper.
- Craft acrylic paints: white and black or glow-in-the-dark paint.
- Aerosol clear acrylic sealer, optional.
- Drill and 1/16" drill bit.
- Lightweight monofilament fishing line.
- Black grosgrain ribbon, ¼" (6 mm) wide).

CUTTING DIRECTIONS

Cut four 2½" (6.5 cm) dowel pieces for the arms. Cut four 3½" (9 cm) dowel pieces for the legs. Cut one 4" (10 cm) dowel piece for the shoulders.

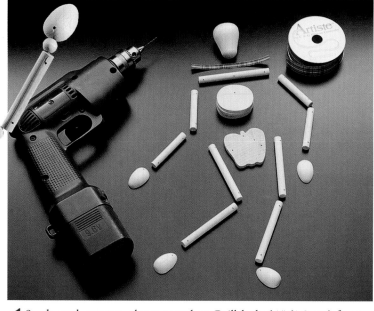

1 Stack oval cutouts; clamp together. Drill hole ½" (1.3 cm) from outer edge of one long side, using 1/16" drill bit. Drill hole ¼" (6 mm) from each end of each dowel piece; drill hole in middle of shoulder piece. Clamp dowel pieces to work surface to be sure all holes are centered and parallel. Drill hole through apple cutout at base of stem; drill hole ¼" (6 mm) from edge at center of each side. Drill hole ¼" (6 mm) from narrow end of two egg shapes for feet; drill hole ¼" (6 mm) from wide end of two egg shapes for hands. Predrill shallow hole in center of narrow end of pear, for screw eye. Repeat at wide end, for hanging skeleton.

2 Sand any rough edges, using 100-grit sandpaper. Paint all pieces as desired. String wooden spools and beads; suspend over shoe box, for ease in painting. Paint skull features; add any other accents as desired. Apply acrylic sealer, if desired.

3 Insert screw eye in narrow end of skull. String skull, neck, shoulders, vertebrae, ribs, and pelvis together as shown, using monofilament line. Run line from top to bottom and back up to top; pull line snug, and knot securely.

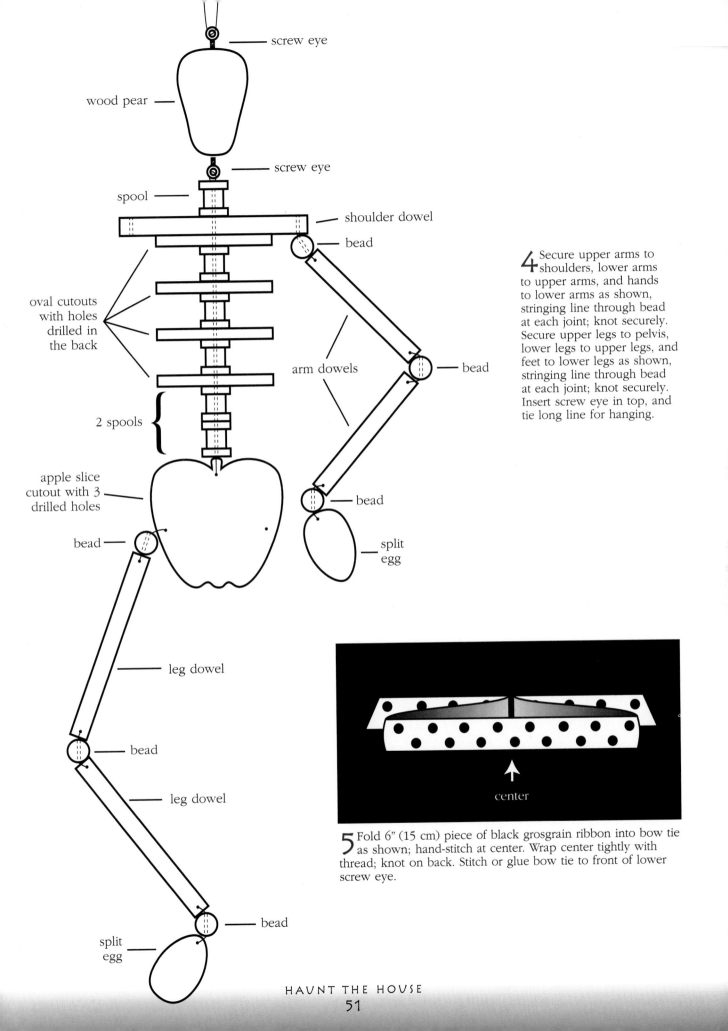

screw eye

wood pear

screw eye

spool

shoulder dowel

bead

oval cutouts
with holes
drilled in
the back

arm dowels

bead

2 spools

apple slice
cutout with 3
drilled holes

bead

split
egg

bead

leg dowel

bead

leg dowel

split
egg

bead

center

4 Secure upper arms to
shoulders, lower arms
to upper arms, and hands
to lower arms as shown,
stringing line through bead
at each joint; knot securely.
Secure upper legs to pelvis,
lower legs to upper legs, and
feet to lower legs as shown,
stringing line through bead
at each joint; knot securely.
Insert screw eye in top, and
tie long line for hanging.

5 Fold 6" (15 cm) piece of black grosgrain ribbon into bow tie
as shown; hand-stitch at center. Wrap center tightly with
thread; knot on back. Stitch or glue bow tie to front of lower
screw eye.

SPIDERWEB MOBILE

This spider has the Halloween spirit! Suspend her fanciful spiderweb in a doorway or from a light fixture where it will delight unsuspecting guests.

Wrap a wooden embroidery hoop with dental floss to form the web. Use various lengths of floss to suspend polymer clay shapes from the web.

Knead polymer clay with your hands for several minutes, until it is pliable enough to form shapes, press into molds, or roll flat for cutting. Clean your hands with a disposable towelette before working with another clay color. Use Halloween candy molds or fashion your own little critters. Ease removal of the clay from candy molds with a very light dusting of baby powder.

HOW TO MAKE A SPIDERWEB MOBILE

MATERIALS

- Wooden embroidery hoop, 10" (25.5 cm) diameter.
- Dental floss tape, for web.
- Mat knife.
- Craft glue.
- Small plastic ring.

- Polymer clay, black and assorted colors.
- Toothpick; aluminum foil.
- Disposable towelettes.
- Baking sheet.

- Assorted candy molds, baby powder, small soft paintbrush, screw eyes, for 3-D shapes.
- Assorted cookie cutters, large dowel, for flat shapes.
- Acrylic paints, optional.

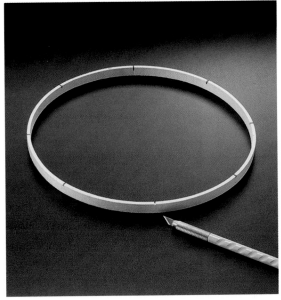

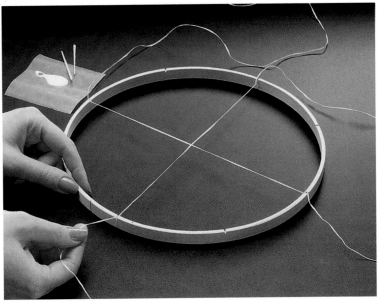

1 Mark eight evenly spaced points about 3⅞" (9.7 cm) apart along top edge of inner hoop. Notch the hoop at each mark, using craft knife.

2 Tie dental floss at two opposing marks, leaving 24" (61 cm) tails for hangers. Repeat at two more opposing marks, forming an "X" through the center. Apply dot of craft glue on knots, using toothpick.

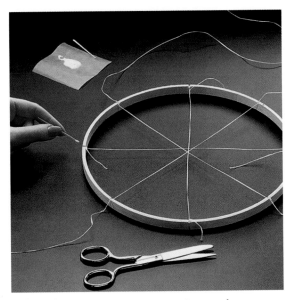

3 Tie floss at remaining opposing marks, forming second "X". Apply dot of glue on each knot; trim excess floss close to knots. Do not trim hanger tails.

4 Tie floss to center intersection, securing all strands together. Wrap floss around one strand, about ⅜" (1 cm) from center. Continue to wrap floss once around each strand of web in a spiral, holding onto previous wrap to prevent it from slipping.

(Continued)

5 Apply glue to each wrap after completing round of eight wraps. Continue wrapping the floss at each strand; glue wraps after each round.

6 Roll two polymer clay balls of ½" and ¼" (1.3 cm and 6 mm) diameter for the spider body. Flatten larger ball slightly on one side and attach smaller ball as shown. Smooth two balls together, using toothpick. Roll small amount of clay into ⅜" (1 cm) long rod, pointing ends; attach to underside of the head, for pincers.

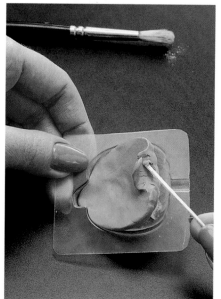

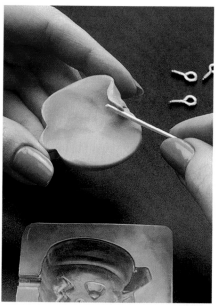

7 Roll clay into four thin rods, about 2¾" (7 cm) long. Align rods; pinch them together at center. Press rods onto center of spider's flat side, for legs. Arrange legs as desired; smooth seams with toothpick. Insert screw eye into belly. Prop spider body on aluminum foil; bake with other shapes.

8 Load small amount of baby powder on artist's brush; dust candy mold. Estimate amount of clay needed to fill candy mold about half full; roll ball. Press ball into general shape; push into mold. Insert tooth-pick gently along edge; gently pry clay from mold.

9 Smooth nicked areas, using tooth-pick; draw with toothpick tip to accentuate details, if desired. Gently insert screw eye at top of shape. Place shapes on baking sheet; bake, following manufacturer's directions.

10 Roll clay flat on clean formica surface. Cut designs, using cookie cutters or knife. Add surface details, using toothpick. Gently poke hole at least ⅛" (3 mm) from top of design. Place shapes on baking sheet; drape over aluminum foil props, if desired. Bake, following manufacturer's directions.

11 Accent baked shapes with paint, if desired. Knot strands of floss to screw eyes and holes in shapes. Attach spider to web. Hang other shapes from web, trimming floss to various lengths. Tie four hanger tails to small plastic ring for hanging.

SHAPE VARIATIONS

Blend two colors of clay well to achieve new colors or partially blend colors to get marbleized surface variations.

Make glow-in-the-dark forms that float mysteriously overhead when the lights go out. Use Fimo® Nite-Glo® clay. Or highlight areas of colorful shapes with glow-in-the-dark paint.

Tie wired felt shapes (page 102) to web with invisible thread.

Tie small purchased ornaments to web.

SCARECROW WALL HANGING

Handsome Mr. Scarecrow has banned all crows from the pumpkin patch in this three-dimensional wall hanging. Some embellishments are included as you piece him together; others, added just before hanging him on a branch, provide lots of ways to make this banner uniquely your own.

The banner is a collection of easily pieced blocks; large background rectangles make it quick to assemble. Fabric scraps are suitable for the entire scarecrow and the pumpkins. Use ¼" (6 mm) seam allowances throughout, stitching at 12 to 15 stitches per inch (2.5 cm).

HOW TO MAKE A SCARECROW WALL HANGING

MATERIALS

- ¼ yd. (0.25 m) fabric, for background.
- ⅛ yd. (0.15 m) each of five fabrics, or assorted scraps, for scarecrow face, clothing, and pumpkins.
- ¼ yd. (0.25 m) fabric, for border.
- Raffia.
- Jute twine.
- ⅝ yd. (0.6 m) fusible batting.
- ⅝ yd. (0.6 m) fabric, for backing.
- Embroidery floss as desired.
- Permanent markers, optional.
- Decorative buttons.
- Fusible web, ⅜" (1 cm) wide.
- Wood fence; assorted wood shapes, optional.
- Tea bag and assorted paints, optional.
- Glue gun and glue sticks, optional.
- Branch, about 30" (76 cm) long.

CUTTING DIRECTIONS

From the background fabric, cut fourteen 1" (2.5 cm) squares; cut two pieces, using the template (page 61). Cut five small rectangles; two 1¼" × 2½" (3.2 × 6.5 cm), one 2½" × 1½" (6.5 × 3.8 cm), one 2½" × 2" (6.5 × 5 cm), and one 1" × 3½" (2.5 × 9 cm). Cut three large rectangles; cut A 4" × 5" (10 × 12.5 cm), cut B 7" × 11½" (18 × 29.3 cm), cut C 6½" × 14½" (16.3 × 36.8 cm). Cut two strips; one 16½" × 2" (41.8 × 5 cm) and one 16½" × 3" (41.8 × 7.5 cm).

Cut two 3¾" × 4½" (9.5 × 11.5 cm) and one 4" × 2½" (10 × 6.5 cm) rectangles from the pants fabric.

Cut one 4" (10 cm) square and one 9" × 3½" (23 × 9 cm) rectangle from the shirt fabric.

Cut one 2½" (6.5 cm) square from the head fabric.

From the hat fabric, cut one 4" × 2" (10 × 5 cm) rectangle; cut one piece, using the hat template (page 61).

From the pumpkin fabric, cut one 2½" (6.5 cm) square and two rectangles; one 2½" × 3½" (6.5 × 9 cm) and one 2½" × 2" (6.5 × 5 cm). Also cut six 3" (7.5 cm) squares and two 3" × 3¾" (7.5 × 9.5 cm) rectangles for padded pumpkins.

Cut seven strips; two 3½" × 18½" (9 × 47.3 cm), two 3½" × 22½" (9 × 57.2 cm) and three 3" × 20" (7.5 × 51 cm) from border fabric.

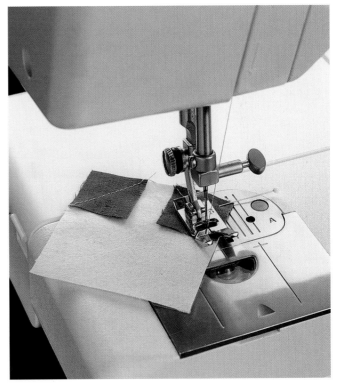

1 Press two pants rectangles in half, wrong sides together, to measure 1⅞" × 4½" (4.7 × 11.5 cm). Pin to right side of large rectangle A; place folds near center and align raw edges at top and sides. Place third pants rectangle, right side down, over legs. Stitch across top, securing both legs; turn third pants rectangle up.

2 Pin 1" (2.5 cm) background squares to bottom corners of head square, right sides together. Stitch diagonally across small squares, corner to corner. Trim seam allowances to ¼" (6 mm); press to make square. Stitch matching background rectangle to each side of head, right sides together; press seam allowances toward background.

(Continued)

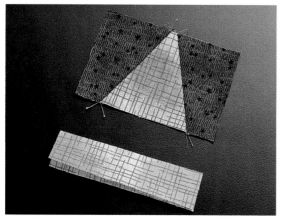

3 Stitch background sections to hat triangle, right sides together, to form 2½" × 4" (6.5 × 10 cm) block; press. Press hat rectangle in half lengthwise, wrong sides together, for brim.

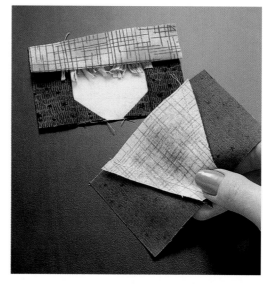

4 Cut raffia pieces about 1" (2.5 cm) long; arrange across top of head. Place brim and then lower edge of hat block over raffia, right sides down and raw edges even with top and sides of head block; pin. Stitch; turn hat up.

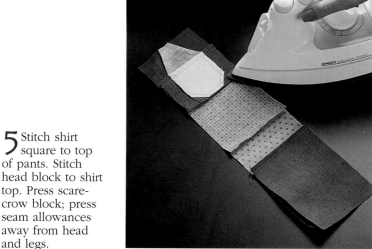

5 Stitch shirt square to top of pants. Stitch head block to shirt top. Press scarecrow block; press seam allowances away from head and legs.

6 Turn brim up about ½" (1.3 cm); pin at sides of block. Knot pieces of twine for belt; pin at waist sides.

7 Pin 1" (2.5 cm) background squares to each corner of three small pumpkin pieces. Stitch; trim and press as on page 57, step 2.

8 Assemble the pumpkin block, using three pumpkin squares and three small background pieces, following diagram on page 61; stitch horizontal seams first, then vertical seams.

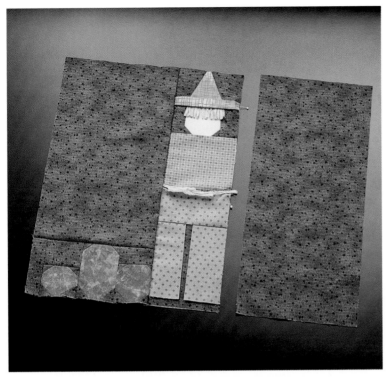

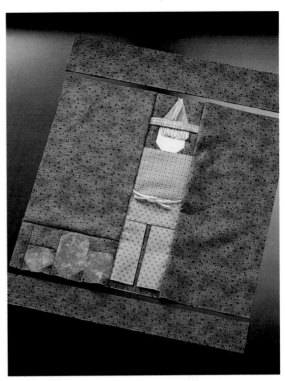

9 Stitch large rectangle B to upper edge of pumpkin block, right sides together; press. Stitch block to left side of scarecrow block. Stitch large rectangle C to right side of scarecrow block; catch ends of belt and hat brim in seams.

10 Pin a few short raffia pieces to hat top. Stitch background strips to top and bottom of pieced unit, catching raffia in top seam. Press entire block; press last seams toward pieced unit.

11 Fold sleeve in half lengthwise; press. Press raw edges under ¼" (6 mm). Place second fold over head block and shirt seam, centering sleeve on body; sleeve will cover face. Pin; stitch on foldline. Press sleeve down.

12 Stitch short border strips to sides of pieced unit; press seam allowances toward borders. Stitch long border strips to top and bottom of unit; press. Bordered unit should measure 22½" × 24½" (57.2 × 62.3 cm).

13 Fuse fleece to wrong side of bordered unit, following manufacturer's directions; trim excess fleece. Fold remaining strips in half crosswise, wrong sides together, forming ties. Pin to right side of unit, aligning fold to upper raw edge; center one tie, and pin others about ½" (1.3 cm) from sides.

(Continued)

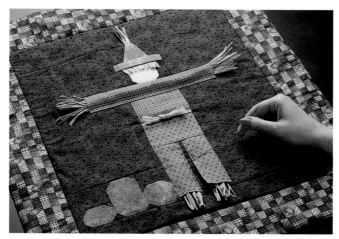

14 Cut backing fabric to same size as bordered unit. Stitch to unit, right sides together, leaving 6" (15 cm) opening along lower edge. Trim corners; turn right side out. Press lightly, turning raw edges in at opening; close with fusible web strip. Stitch in the ditch around border.

15 Glue 5½" (14 cm) raffia lengths under pants legs. Tuck 12½" (31.8 cm) raffia lengths under sleeve. Secure folded edges of legs and sleeve to background, using running stitch and two strands embroidery floss.

17 Make padded pumpkins in various shapes and sizes, following steps 1 and 2 on page 89. Add stems to all pumpkins with embroidery floss. Layer fleece between two fabric pieces for pumpkin patch sign. Press to fuse one fabric piece; use running stitch or glue to secure other piece. Attach sign to stick; sew or glue stick to banner.

16 Embellish scarecrow as desired. Draw or embroider face. Fuse small patches to clothing. Add buttons for clothing details.

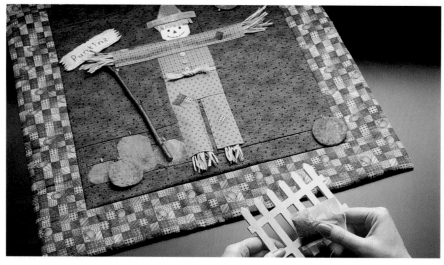

18 Stain the wooden shapes, using wet tea bag, or paint as desired; attach to the banner. Sew decorative buttons to banner as desired. Attach padded pumpkins. Knot ties over branch; trim excess length.

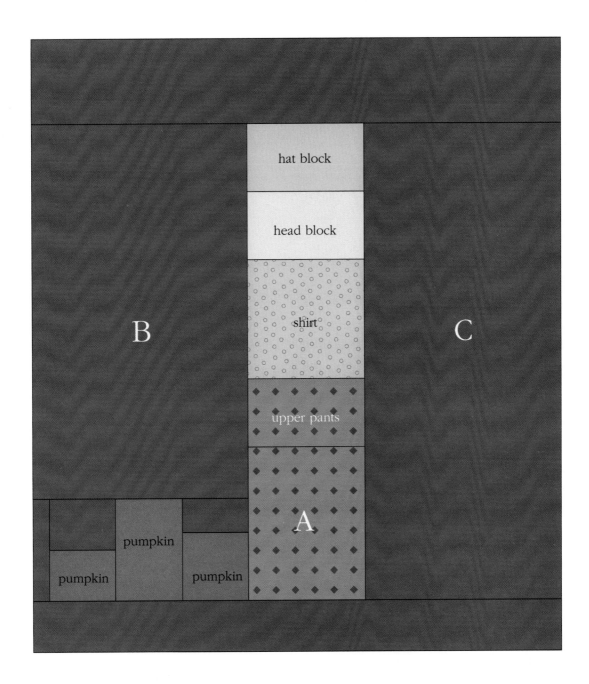

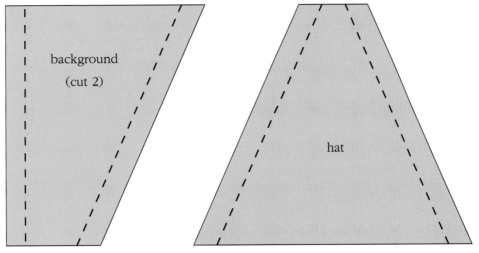

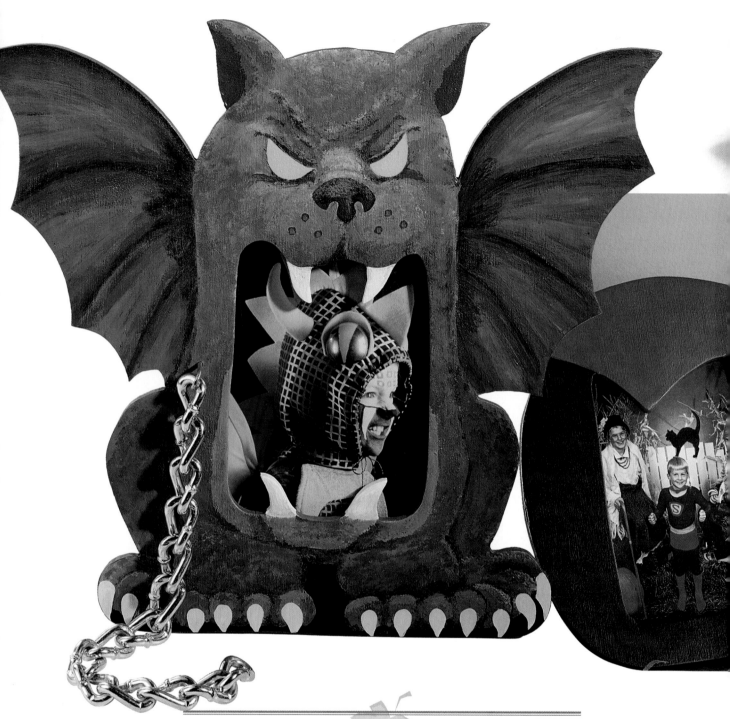

PICTURE FRAMES

Display photos of your favorite Halloween ghouls 'n guys in wooden picture frames you make yourself. Design any shape, allowing adequate space beyond the opening for a backing board. Stand frames with a level bottom edge on a table. Plan symmetrical designs for hanging frames on a wall, or adjust the placement of the hanger to allow the frame to hang straight. Cut openings to fit standard 5" × 7" (12.5 × 18 cm) or 4" × 6" (10 × 15 cm) photos.

Paint, stain, stencil, and embellish the frames in a variety of ways. Use Paper Etch® for a wood-burned effect, or glue wood cutouts, buttons, or polymer clay shapes to the frame surface.

MATERIALS

- Finish-grade ¼" (6 mm) plywood or poplar board.
- Glass, 5" × 7" (12.5 × 18 cm).
- Drill and ¼" drill bit.
- Coping saw or jigsaw.
- Hardboard, ⅛" (3 mm) thick.
- 220-grit sandpaper.

- Wood glue.
- Craft sticks, for spacers.
- Drive-in picture hanger, for hanging frame.
- Easel, 5" × 7" (12.5 × 18 cm) for standing frame.

- Materials for finishing and decorating frames, such as acrylic paints, water-based wood stain, Paper Etch, aerosol acrylic sealer, wood cutouts, polymer clay shapes, or Halloween buttons.
- Hot glue gun and glue sticks, optional.

HOW TO MAKE A PICTURE FRAME

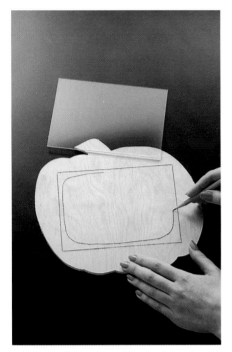

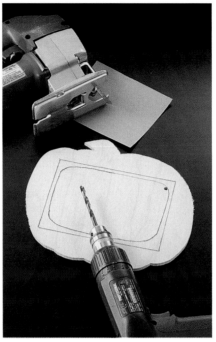

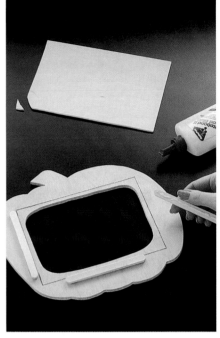

1 Trace desired outline on board; cut out shape, using jigsaw or coping saw. Center glass on back of board, near lower edge and parallel to sides; trace outer edge. Mark cutting line for opening at least ¼" (6 mm) inside traced line, shaping as desired.

2 Drill hole for inserting saw blade just inside marked line; more than one hole may be necessary. Cut away opening, using jigsaw. Sand opening and outer edges, using 220-grit sandpaper.

3 Cut backing from hardboard, allowing ½" (1.3 cm) on three sides to extend beyond glass; trim corners, if necessary. Glue two craft sticks together for each spacer; cut to desired length. Secure spacers to frame back just beyond bottom and side glass lines, using wood glue.

4 Secure backing over spacers, using wood glue; align sides and lower edge of backing to outer edges of spacers. Weight with books until dry.

5 Glue easel to back of standing frame, with lower edge of easel near lower edge of frame. Trim easel, if necessary. Or install picture hanger at top center of backing for symmetrical hanging frame; install a hanger at each upper corner for asymmetrical frames. Paint or decorate frame as desired.

TIPS FOR DECORATING FRAMES

Paint frame, using craft acrylic paints; seal with aerosol acrylic sealer, if desired. Attach wooden cutouts, Halloween charms, or buttons, using hot glue. Snip off button shank, using wire cutter. Make polymer clay shapes (pages 54 and 55). Sand back flat, if necessary. Adhere to surface of frame, using hot glue gun.

Draw design features, using Paper Etch®; follow the manufacturer's directions. Stain frame, using light-colored water-based wood stain. Finish with aerosol acrylic sealer.

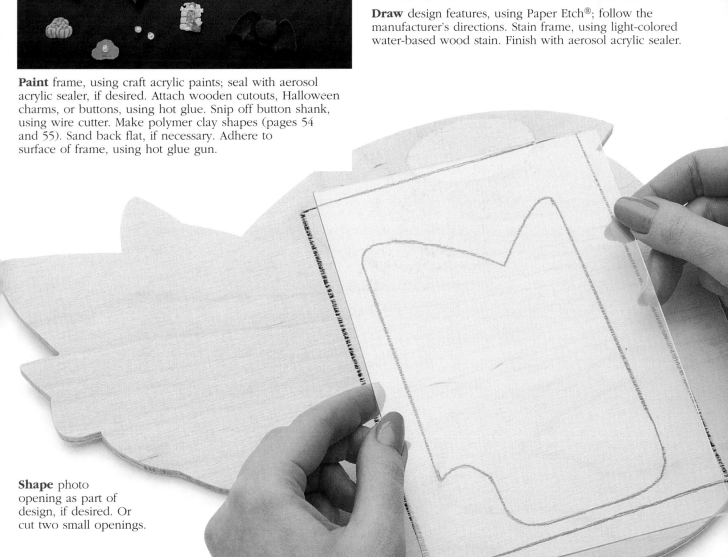

Shape photo opening as part of design, if desired. Or cut two small openings.

HAUNTED BIRDHOUSES

Watch for friendly spirits to move into this once lovely old mansion. Simply transform a birdhouse and set it on a small hill with a rickety picket fence; the spirits will beckon you from behind shuttered windows and welcome you at the door.

Choose from many birdhouse styles available at craft stores for just the mansion you want. A tall, slim house resembles a stately mansion; one with slanted sides appears empty and tumbledown. Select from special shapes like a barn or log cabin, or look for interesting details like tiered roofs and multiple openings.

Use a crackle medium to imitate old, weathered paint, and age the mansion with a light rubbing of dark stain. Draw

unique features such as mullions and faces on the windows, or add slats and knobs to the shutters, using fine-tip brushes or opaque markers. Hang shutters at odd angles and stretch purchased cobwebs between jutting details, if desired.

Create three-dimensional inhabitants for the house, following the directions for wired felt place cards (page 102). Purchase precut wood shapes or dollhouse miniatures to decorate the sides of the house.

Consider various ways to decorate the mansion's hillside landscape. Build a tumbledown fence, add barren trees and tombstones, and scatter small leaves, if desired.

HOW TO MAKE A HAUNTED BIRDHOUSE

MATERIALS

- Craft birdhouse.
- Drill; ½" drill bit.
- ½" (1.3 cm) dowel.
- Wood glue.
- Acrylic paints; artist's brushes.
- Crackle medium.

- Dark stain; rag; rubber gloves, optional.
- Balsa wood, ¹⁄₁₆" and ⅛" (1.5 and 3 mm) thick.
- Straightedge; mat knife; cutting surface.
- 1 yd. (0.95 m) acetate lining fabric, black.
- Embellishments as desired; hot glue gun.

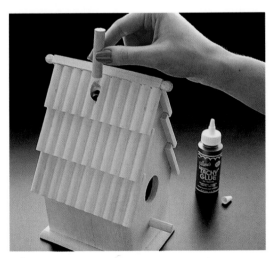

1 Drill hole through birdhouse roof at desired chimney location, using ½" drill bit; drill hole at slight angle if tumbledown chimney is desired. Cut 2" (5 cm) dowel length. Apply glue to inner rim of hole; secure dowel in place. Allow glue to dry.

2 Paint birdhouse with base colors as desired. Apply second coat; allow to dry. Apply even, light coat of crackle medium; allow to set, following manufacturer's directions.

3 Apply single coat of contrasting paint; paint will crackle soon after it is applied. Allow to dry. Rub stain lightly over entire house, using cloth; apply stain more heavily to some areas to show extra wear.

(Continued)

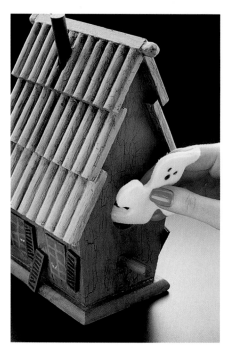

4 Cut windows in desired shapes and sizes from ¹⁄₁₆" (1.5 mm) balsa wood. Cut shutters from ¹⁄₈" (3 mm) balsa wood. Paint and stain as desired; allow to dry. Attach windows and shutters, using hot glue. Allow to hang at odd angles, if desired.

5 Decorate the front entry as desired; position a wired felt shape (page 102) in entry hole. Suspend another wired felt shape over house, wrapping wire around chimney or eave. Add other embellishments as desired.

6 Form hill, using box and aluminum foil; tape crumpled foil near edges, and slope to table surface. Cover hill with fleece or batting.

7 Wet black fabric; twist and roll into ball. Allow to dry. Unroll fabric, and drape over hill; tuck raw edges under. Place house on hill. Make picket fence as shown opposite; position fence around house.

9 Embellish hill as desired. Purchase trees or make trees from twigs. Cut small headstones from balsa wood; spray with fleckstone paint, if desired, and secure to front of small rocks, using hot glue. Attach cobwebs, if desired.

HOW TO MAKE A PICKET FENCE

MATERIALS

- Craft sticks; scissors.
- Hot glue gun.

- Mat knife, optional.
- 5/16" (7.5 mm) dowel; one 3/8" (1 cm) button plug for each fence post.

- Paint; stain; applicators.

1 Use scissors to cut near center of craft stick tip. Break stick in half lengthwise; allow break to follow wood grain for irregular shapes. Use warped and knotted sticks for added interest. Full lengths will be used for horizontal rails; broken sticks for vertical stiles.

2 Position two uneven rows of rails on surface, about 1" (2.5 cm) apart, so total length is 3" to 4" (7.5 to 10 cm) longer than house side. Repeat for each fence section and gate. Arrange stiles on rails at various angles. Use short stiles for broken sections; avoid placing stiles at end of rails.

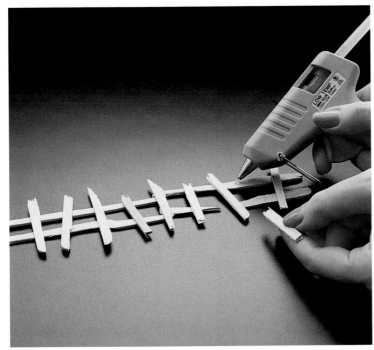

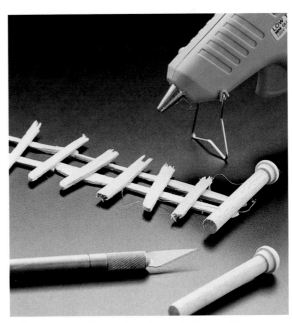

3 Glue stiles to rails, one at a time, using hot glue.

4 Cut 2¼" (6 cm) dowel length for each post; glue button plug to top of each post. Glue posts to rails at corners and ends. Trim excess glue from fence, if necessary, using mat knife. Paint or stain as desired.

BEANBAG PUMPKINS

Perch these jaunty pumpkins on a shelf or mantel, and let another beguile your guests from a wreath or swag. Give them various facial expressions, from friendly grins to menacing scowls.

Make several beanbags from ¼ yd. (0.25 m) of pumpkin fabric. Or use scraps, about 7" (18 cm) square, to make just one. Stuff the top of the bag with fiberfill so your pumpkin won't wilt, and weight the seat with small plastic pellets. Substitute a mesh bag of cloves, grated whole nutmeg, and cinnamon stick pieces for the pellets, and enjoy an inviting "pumpkin pie" aroma.

HOW TO MAKE A BEANBAG PUMPKIN

MATERIALS

- ¼ yd. (0.25 m) fabric, for pumpkin.
- ⅛ yd. (0.15 m) fabric, for arms and legs.
- Small fabric scraps, for face.
- Paper-backed fusible web.
- Erasable marking pen or pencil, optional.
- Polyester fiberfill.
- Plastic pellets.

CUTTING DIRECTIONS

Cut two pumpkins from the pumpkin fabric, using the pattern on page 118. Mark the placement lines on the right side of one piece.

Cut two 2" × 9½" (5 × 24.3 cm) strips for the arms and two 2" × 14½" (5 × 36.8 cm) strips for the legs from contrasting fabric. Cut one 2¼" × 2" (6 × 5 cm) piece for the stem.

Draw or trace facial features on the paper side of fusible web. Fuse it to the scraps, and cut out.

1 Fold arm strip in half lengthwise, right sides together. Mark point **(a)** along fold 1¼" (3.2 cm) from short end. Mark point **(b)** on long cut edge, 1¼" (3.2 cm) from short end and ¼" (6 mm) in from cut edge. Mark point **(c)** ⅜" (1 cm) from fold, ¼" (6 mm) from short end. Draw curved line connecting points. Repeat for remaining arm strip and both leg strips.

(Continued)

2 Stitch ¼" (6 mm) from long edge, following marked line for shaped end. Trim seam allowances on shaped end. Turn right side out. Repeat for remaining strips.

3 Drop a few plastic pellets into foot; tie knot for ankle about 2" (5 cm) from end. Drop in more pellets; tie knot for knee halfway between ankle knot and opening. Repeat for remaining leg.

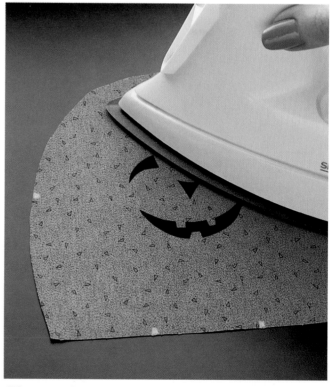

4 Repeat step 3 for arm, tying wrist knot 1½" (3.8 cm) from end; tie elbow knot halfway between wrist and opening. Repeat for remaining arm.

5 Arrange facial features on pumpkin as desired; nose should be even with or just above arm placement marks. Fuse according to manufacturer's directions.

6 Fold the stem in half lengthwise, right sides together; stitch ¼" (6 mm) seam. Turn right side out; press. Fold the stem in half crosswise, aligning cut ends. Pin to right side of pumpkin at center of upper edge. Pin arms and legs at the placement marks, aligning raw edges.

7 Pin second pumpkin piece to first, right sides together; tuck legs and arms inside. Stitch, using ¼" (6 mm) seam allowance; leave 2" (5 cm) opening between legs.

9 Trim seam allowance to a scant ⅛" (3 mm), or clip at ¼" (6 mm) intervals. Turn; smooth seams with fingers. Stuff upper pumpkin firmly with fiberfill; fill bottom with plastic pellets. Hand-stitch opening closed.

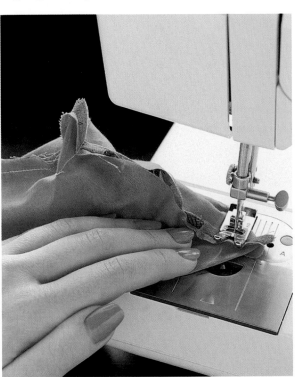

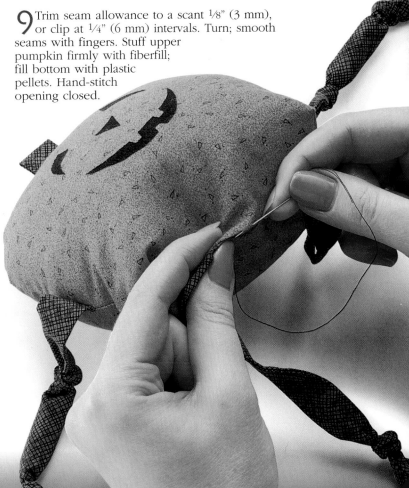

8 Open and fold lower corners so side and bottom seams are aligned. Stitch across corners, at right angle to seams, about ¾" (2 cm) from corners; avoid catching legs or arms in seams.

WOODEN SHELF SITTERS

This collection of shelf sitters will happily watch over your holiday observations. Create your favorite characters and scatter them throughout the house or gather them together to impart their own special magic.

Purchase inexpensive 2 × 2 nominal lumber, which actually measures 1¾" × 1¾" (4.5 × 4.5 cm), for their bodies. Use various precut wood shapes such as square blocks, round balls, and inverted pears for their heads. Join shelf sitter parts after drilling holes in adjacent pieces; clamp small pieces to a work surface to ensure centered and parallel holes, and for safety.

Consider a character's special traits before embellishing. Purchase small precut wood shapes for unique details. "Dress" shelf sitters in appropriate colors and give them cheerful faces, using acrylic paints. Use simple modeling techniques or purchase molds to form clay hands, boots, or special details. Suspend hands and feet inside sleeves and pants that require only a few seams.

HOW TO MAKE A FRANKENSTEIN SHELF SITTER

MATERIALS

- 2 × 2 nominal pine.
- 1¼" (3.2 cm) square wood block, for head.
- ⅝" × ¾" (1.5 × 2 cm) spool, for neck.
- 3⁄16" (4.5 mm) dowel.
- Saw; clamp.
- Drill; 5⁄16", 3⁄16" drill bits; masking tape.
- Acrylic paints, colors as desired.
- Two ¼" (6 mm) wood blocks, for neck nodes.

- Wood glue.
- Fake fur scrap, for hair, optional.
- Polymer clay; craft mold for 1½" (3.8 cm) hands; baby powder; artist's knife; toothpick; small screw eyes; baking sheet.
- ⅛ yd. (0.15 m) fabric; safety pin.
- ¾ yd. (0.7 m) cording.

CUTTING DIRECTIONS

Cut one 4" (10 cm) piece of 2 × 2 pine board, for the body.

Cut one 1½" (3.8 cm) piece of dowel, for the neck.

Cut one 5" × 15" (12.5 × 38 cm) fabric strip, for the legs.
Cut one 5" × 9" (12.5 × 23 cm) fabric strip, for the arms.
Cut cording in two lengths of 11" and 16" (28 and 40.5 cm).

1 Mark center of one end on body and head. Mark two points on body front, ⅜" (1 cm) up from bottom and in from side. Mark point on body side, ¾" (2 cm) down from top and in from back. Drill hole at end marks to ⅜" (1 cm) depth, using 3⁄16" drill bit; wrap masking tape around drill bit as guide for depth. Drill holes through body at front and side marks, using 5⁄16" drill bit.

(Continued)

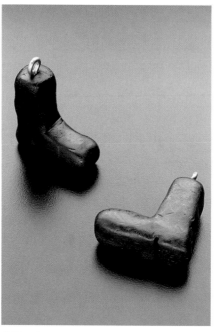

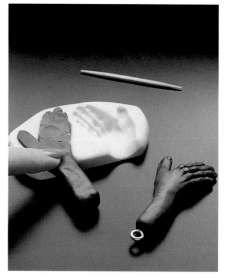

2 Paint body, head, neck, and two neck nodes. Allow to dry; paint facial features as desired. Paint hair, or secure fake fur scrap on head, using glue. Secure neck nodes to each side of neck, using glue; secure dowel in each end hole, positioning face as desired. Allow to dry.

3 Soften clay for boot, following general directions on page 52. Roll clay ball into fat 2" (5 cm) long cylinder. Gently fold one-third of cylinder under, forming boot front. Shape boot as desired; mark heel gently with knife side. Insert screw eye into top as shown. Repeat for second boot.

4 Soften clay for hands. Press clay ball into approximate mold shape; place in lightly dusted mold. Push clay into fingertips; push clay beyond mold edges, and extend arm about 1" (2.5 cm) beyond wrist. Gently lift hand from mold; remove excess clay, using knife tip. Roll toothpick along edges to smooth; use tip to add or accentuate details. Gently cup palm. Insert screw eyes into arm ends. Bake boots and hands, following manufacturer's directions.

5 Turn under ¼" (6 mm) on each short end of fabric strip; edgestitch. Fold strip in half lengthwise, right sides together; stitch ¼" (6 mm) seam. Turn tube right side out, using safety pin. Repeat with other strip. Gather ends slightly, using hand stitches.

6 Thread short cord through short tube, using safety pin. Insert tube through side hole, for sleeves. Tie cord ends to hands, adjusting position of hand in the sleeve as desired; trim the cord. Thread long cord through long tube for pants; insert legs through holes from back. Secure boots.

VARIATIONS FOR SHELF SITTERS

Purchase wooden balls or pears *(below) for the head. Use ⁵/₁₆"*
drill bit to drill holes; join head and body with a ⁵/₁₆" (7.5 mm)
dowel. Secure braided wool hair or bits of yarn or raffia for
delightful hairdos, using glue. Use fabric scraps or doll clothes for
capes, hats, or scarves.

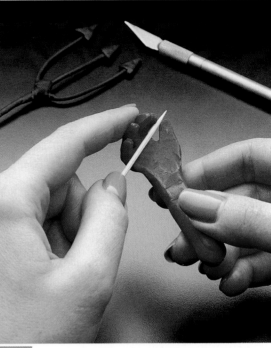

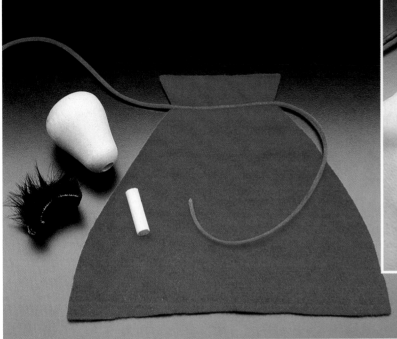

Cut between clay fingers *(above);*
separate and shape them slightly as
desired. Or curl the palm gently around
toothpick; secure small item in hand after
baking, using all-purpose adhesive.

Sew a third fabric tube *(below) for a tail;*
knot end around leg fabric at back. To pose
a character's arms, legs, or tail, substitute
chenille stems for the cording.

Apply transparent stain, *instead of paint, to allow the wood grain*
to show on natural characters such as scarecrows and pumpkins.

Worms
and
Beetles

Eye of
Newt

Dragon's
Stew

Fill cauldron
full with Beetles.
Add two handfuls
of white worms. Sti...

HARLEQUIN TABLE RUNNER

This easy-to-sew pointed harlequin table runner makes a beautiful backdrop for Halloween appliqué motifs. The finished size is about 51" × 18½" (129.5 × 47.3 cm). Lengthen the runner, if desired, by adding diagonal rows of blocks.

This runner uses the easiest of sewing methods. Cut fabric squares and strips with a rotary cutter and mat,

for greatest efficiency. A 6" (15 cm) wide transparent straightedge makes it easy to cut accurately. Stitch ¼" (6 mm) seams, using a short stitch length.

Simple Halloween appliqués are fused to the runner. You may prefer to substitute pumpkins, flying witches, ghosts, or ravens for the black cat. Edgestitch around the appliqués to give them interesting dimension.

HOW TO MAKE A HARLEQUIN TABLE RUNNER

MATERIALS

- ³⁄₈ yd. (0.35 m) fabric A, for outer rows of squares.
- ¼ yd. (0.25 m) fabric B, for center squares.
- ¼ yd. (0.25 m) fabric C, for outer triangles.
- ¾ yd. (0.7 m) fabric, for backing.
- ¼ yd. (0.25 m) fabric, for border.
- Batting, about 20" × 54" (51 × 137 cm).
- ¼ yd. (0.25 m) black fabric, for cats, or suitable fabric scraps, for appliqués.
- Paper-backed fusible web.
- Straightedge.

CUTTING DIRECTIONS

Cut ten 6" (15 cm) squares from fabric A, six 6" (15 cm) squares from fabric B, and four 6³⁄₈" (16 cm) squares from fabric C. Cut fabric C squares diagonally to make eight triangles.

Cut four 2" (5 cm) strips across the width of the border fabric.

1 Stitch six A squares to six B squares, right sides together, stitching along one side. Stitch four remaining A squares to opposite sides of the same B squares, right sides together. You will have two A-B rows and four A-B-A rows.

(Continued)

2 Arrange rows diagonally. Place triangles at ends of rows as shown. Stitch triangles to ends of rows. Press all seam allowances toward A squares.

3 Stitch the rows together; seam allowances alternate in opposite directions at intersecting seams. Press; avoid stretching bias edges of triangles. Measure sides; cut two border strips equal to shorter measurement plus ½" (1.3 cm).

4 Pin border strips to sides. Stitch, easing as necessary; press seams toward border. Lay straight edge along diagonal end of runner; trim border strip end. Repeat on remaining ends of border strips.

5 Cut border strip equal to length of one diagonal edge plus ½" (1.3 cm). Pin strip to runner, aligning one end to runner point; strip extends past side strip. Stitch; press. Repeat for adjoining diagonal edge. Repeat for opposite end. Trim the end strips even with side strips.

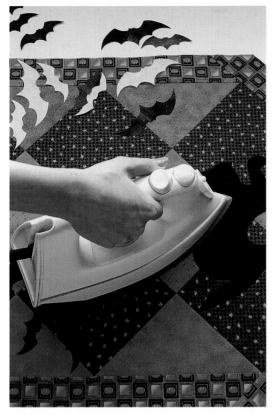

6 Trace Halloween motifs on paper side of fusible web; fuse to motif fabric, following manufacturer's directions. Cut out motifs; remove paper, and fuse to runner.

7 Seam backing fabric as necessary to measure about 20" × 54" (51 × 137 cm). Cut fabric the shape of the runner, using pieced top as pattern. Layer pieced top and backing, right sides together and all edges aligned, over batting; pin all around.

8 Stitch around outer edge, pivoting at corners; leave 6" (15 cm) opening on one side. Trim batting close to stitching; trim even with fabric at opening. Turn. Press lightly, tucking seam allowances in; pin opening closed.

9 Edgestitch around border. Stitch in the ditch between rows of blocks and around border. Edgestitch around appliqué motifs.

PUMPKIN TABLE LINENS

This easy-to-sew set of table linens clearly emphasizes the traditional Halloween pumpkin, and it is just as appropriate for the whole harvest season. Create the entire set or select your favorite parts to delight your dinner guests.

Padded placemats are embellished with a stem and leaves. Top-stitched pumpkin ribs and leaf veins add interesting dimension. An optional paper twist tendril is removed for laundering.

For simplicity and minimal expense, the table runner is made from the full width of fabric. The runner and napkins feature fused appliqués. They may be embellished with hand sewing or fabric paint. Allow paints to dry 24 hours before use and 72 hours before laundering. Any raffia bows or tassels at the points of the table runner should be removed before laundering.

Placemats, table runner, and napkins (left) *set a cozy country table for daily family meals. Or bring them out for special autumn occasions. Surprise your guests with spiderweb coasters* (above).

MATERIALS

For one table runner, four placemats, four napkins, and four coasters:

- ½ yd. (0.5 m) fabric, for table runner.
- 1⅝ yd. (1.5 m) fabric, for pumpkin shell.
- ⅜ yd. (0.35 m) fabric, for leaves and stems.
- Polyester or cotton batting; 28" × 38" (71 × 96.5 cm) for placemats and 5" (12.5 cm) square scraps for coasters.
- Tracing paper, 14" × 19" (35.5 × 48.5 cm).
- Erasable marking pen or pencil.
- Paper-backed fusible web.
- Fusible web, ⅜" (1 cm) wide.
- Green paper twist with wire core, optional.
- 1 yd. (0.95 m) fabric, for napkins.
- Embroidery floss, orange, green, black, optional.
- Dimensional fabric paints, optional.
- ¼ yd. (0.25 m) fabric or 5" (12.5 cm) square scraps, for coasters.
- Raffia, plastic spiders, optional.

CUTTING DIRECTIONS

For the table runner, fold the fabric crosswise, aligning the selvages. Trim both edges as necessary so they are at right angles to the selvages. Cut away the selvages.

For the placemats, fold tracing paper into fourths; unfold. Trace the pattern (page 119) in one quadrant. Refold the paper; cut on the marked line through all layers to make a full pattern.

Cut the pumpkin shells; eight from fabric, four from batting.

Cut 3½" × 5" (9 × 12.5 cm) rectangles for the stems; eight from fabric, four from batting.

Cut 5" (12.5 cm) squares for leaves; sixteen from fabric, eight from batting.

For the napkins, cut four 18" (46 cm) squares.

For the coasters, cut eight 5" (12.5 cm) fabric squares and four 5" (12.5 cm) batting squares.

HOW TO MAKE A PUMPKIN PLACEMAT

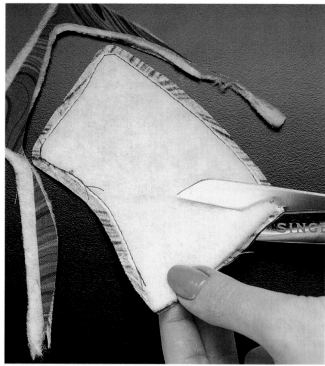

1 Trace and cut out stem pattern (page 119). Transfer pattern outline to wrong side of one fabric rectangle. Layer two rectangles, right sides together, over batting rectangle, with pattern outline on top. Stitch on marked line, leaving bottom open. Trim batting close to stitching; trim fabric to scant ¼" (6 mm) from stitching and on bottom line. Clip curves. Turn right side out; press lightly. Edgestitch seamlines.

2 Trace, cut, and transfer leaf pattern, as in step 1; cut 2" (5 cm) slit at center of one shape. Layer fabric squares and batting, as in step 1. Stitch along entire line. Trim batting and fabric, as in step 1; clip at pivot points and along curves. Turn leaf right side out through slit; press lightly. Slip 2¼" (6 cm) fusible web strip inside slit; fuse closed. Stitch leaf veins. Edgestitch, stretching edge slightly to curve. Repeat for second leaf.

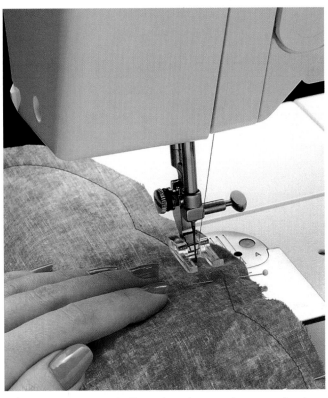

3 Staystitch ½" (1.3 cm) from the upper edge of both pumpkin shell pieces for about 5" (12.5 cm), pivoting at indentations. Mark ribs on right side of one shell with erasable marker.

4 Layer pumpkin shells, right sides together, over batting; pin. Stitch ½" (1.3 cm) seam allowance; backstitch at each end of staystitching, leaving 5" (12.5 cm) opening.

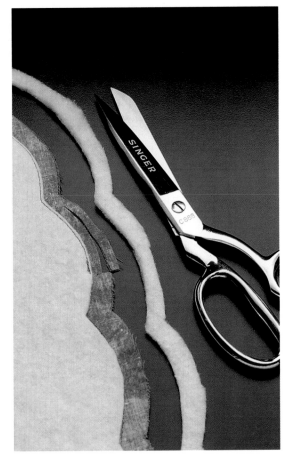

5 Trim batting close to stitching and even with staystitching along opening. Trim fabric seam allowance to scant ¼" (6 mm); leave opening untrimmed. Clip to stitching at each pivot point; clip all around shell at ½" (1.3 cm) intervals. Turn; press lightly, turning under seam allowances of opening.

6 Insert stem ¾" (2 cm) into opening; pin. Edgestitch placemat, catching stem and closing opening. Stitch on marked rib lines. Tack leaves loosely to top of pumpkin. Wrap paper twist around pencil to create tendril, if desired. Slip tendril under leaf, between tacking.

HOW TO MAKE A TABLE RUNNER

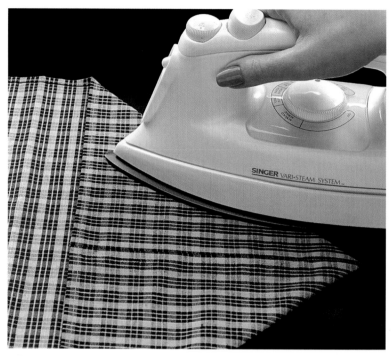

1 Press under ¼" (6 mm) twice on long sides; stitch to make double-fold hems.

2 Fold runner in half lengthwise, right sides together; pin ends. Stitch ¼" (6 mm) seams at both ends. Press seams open. Turn right side out, and position seam at center of runner; press diagonal folds.

HOW TO MAKE A HALLOWEEN NAPKIN

1 Press under ½" (1.3 cm) on each side of the fabric square. Unfold corner; fold diagonally so pressed folds are aligned. Press diagonal fold; trim corner.

2 Fold raw edges under ¼" (6 mm). Press double-fold hem in place. Stitch close to inner fold, pivoting at mitered corners.

3 Fuse and embellish small pumpkin and stem near napkin corner, as for table runner, steps 3 and 4.

3 Trace medium pumpkin and stem twice on paper side of paper-backed fusible web. Fuse to fabrics, following manufacturer's directions. Cut out pumpkins and stems; fuse near table runner ends.

4 Draw four ribs on pumpkins with erasable marker. Hand-stitch running stitches along ribs, using one strand of embroidery floss. Backstitch tendrils, using three strands of floss. Or outline pumpkins, ribs, and stems with fabric paint. Pin raffia bows or tassels at points, if desired.

HOW TO MAKE A COASTER

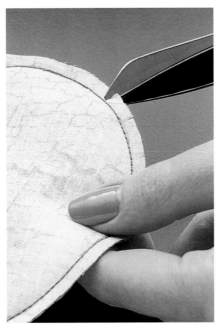

1 Draw 4½" (11.5 cm) circle on wrong side of one fabric square. Slit fabric for about 1½" (3.8 cm) at circle center. Layer fabrics, right sides together, on batting. Stitch on line.

2 Trim batting close to stitching. Trim fabric to scant ¼" (6 mm); clip seam allowance at ½" (1.3 cm) intervals. Turn, press, and fuse slit closed as for pumpkin leaf (page 86).

3 Stitch web spokes from edge to edge, using contrasting thread; backstitch at edge. Stitch three circles of connecting web lines as shown. Tack plastic spider to coaster side, if desired.

PAINTED GLASS SERVERS

Serve Halloween treats on a variety of hand-painted glass dishes. Use basic techniques and special acrylic paints developed for use on glass or tile, or mix a glass medium into acrylic craft paints.

Select heat-set glass and tile paints to decorate tempered glass dishes. Select air-dry enamels or modify craft paints when it is not possible to determine if the glass is tempered; air-dry ten days before use.

Avoid painting surfaces that will come in contact with food or be put in mouths, even if the paints are nontoxic. Experiment with paints to determine their translucency; modified craft paints and some glass paint brands are more opaque.

Plan a design on a paper pattern, if desired. Consider how the dish will be viewed; paint mirror images on the underside of plates and trays or when letters and designs will be viewed from inside containers like bowls and stemware.

Create a stencil for very clean edges; limit stencil designs to a single color, as stencil adhesives may lift the paints. Or paint designs freehand. Apply paint using artist's brushes and household items to achieve a carefree look. Apply paint using sponges for a dappled effect.

MATERIALS

- Glass serving dishes.
- Paper; tape.
- Isopropyl alcohol, lint-free cloth.
- Air-dry or heat-set glass and tile paints, or acrylic paints and glass medium; brushes.
- Newspaper; wood blocks.
- Small dowels; craft bottles with tip set, optional.
- Removable tape, self-adhesive vinyl, mat knife, and cutting surface, for stencil painting.
- Cellulose or sea sponges, for sponge painting.

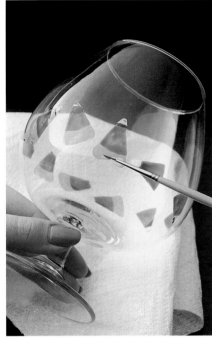

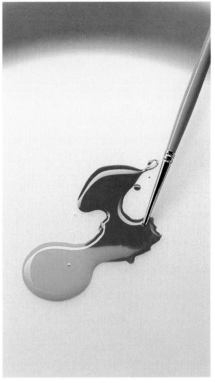

Consider design and determine colors that sit on top or in front of other colors; paint these colors first. When two colors abut a third, paint the center one first; both sides may be painted without requiring extra drying time.

Raise the glass toward a light; look for consistency of coverage to determine if a second coat is desired; allow thirty minutes between coats. Allow paint to dry thoroughly before applying background colors, to avoid lifting foreground colors off the glass.

Create unique colors by blending colors of any one manufacturer; avoid blending colors from different manufacturers.

Apply thin lines of paint using accent liner, or fill craft bottle with paint and use small-tip cap.

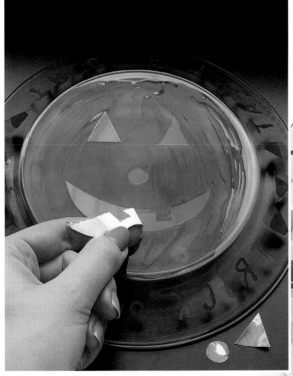

Mask design areas, using self-adhesive vinyl. Remove vinyl immediately after painting.

HOW TO PAINT A DESIGN

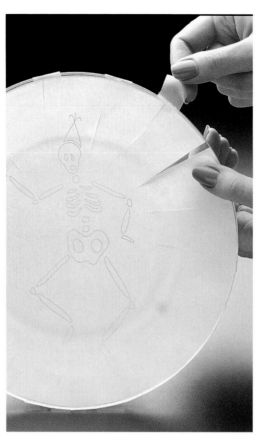

1 Mark general shape of glass item on paper; trace outer edges of nearly flat items, or draw rectangle with dimensions equal to height and circumference of curved items. Draw design within shape. Wash glass well in hot, soapy water; dry. Wipe glass with isopropyl alcohol, using lint-free cloth. Place pattern face-down on right side of item, positioning as desired. Cut the pattern as necessary, lapping paper to fit item without distorting design details; tape.

2 Turn item over, or rest it on its side; place on newspaper. Apply as many foreground colors as possible; apply second coat, if necessary. Allow paint to dry thoroughly.

3 Paint adjacent colors, lapping first colors slightly; apply second coats, if necessary. Dry thoroughly. Continue until entire pattern is painted.

4 Dip brush handle tip into paint to apply small, slightly irregular dots of color. Use dowel ends of various sizes for larger, more perfect paint circles. Cut motifs from cellulose sponges. Dip sponge into paint puddle; blot on newspaper to remove excess paint. Press sponge evenly on flat surfaces, or roll sponge across curved surfaces.

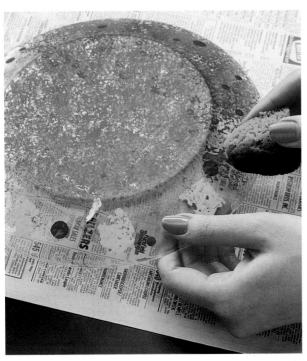

5 Dip sea sponge into paint; blot on newspaper. Dab paint on glass, turning and rotating sponge to avoid repetition of sponge pattern.

6 Prop glass on wood blocks and paint entire bottom or outside of dish, if desired. Cure, following manufacturer's directions. Apply two coats of clear gloss or satin glaze to improve durability of painted designs; allow one hour between coats. Cure well before washing.

HOW TO MAKE & USE A STENCIL

1 Clean glass and draw design as in step 1, opposite. Tape design to light source, such as light table or window; place right side up for lettered designs that will be read on the top or inside of a dish; place down for designs with lettering that will be read on the outside of the dish. Trace design onto paper backing of self-adhesive vinyl.

2 Cut vinyl on design lines, using mat knife. Remove paper backing carefully. Press vinyl to the glass, smoothing vinyl from center to outer edges; clip and lap vinyl where necessary. Press all vinyl edges firmly for secure grip; avoid touching glass. Apply paint; apply second coat, if necessary. Remove stencil immediately after painting. Allow paint to dry thoroughly.

...I shrieked, the
Get thee back into the
Night's Plutonian shore!
plumage as a token of that lie
spoken! Leave my
loneliness unbroken! quit the
first above beak from
Take thy out my heart, and take
thy form off my door!"
"Quoth the Raven,
"Nevermore"

Edgar Allen Poe

BOO

TREAT BAG INVITATIONS

Deliver these invitations to your guests in person, or if they're away, leave a bag on a doorknob to brighten their return. Advise them to bring the invitation to the party and they'll go home with a bag full of treats!

Select small gift or craft bags that have handles, or cut handles in ordinary lunch bags. This is a fun project for children of all ages; just gather the materials and each invitation will be unique.

Consider the variety of ways to decorate a bag, as shown on these pages, and choose the one you like best. Combine methods for even more variety. Cut silhouettes from the bag and insert colored paper backing. Create a fabric collage on a quilted fabric, and complete the design using trims, buttons, decorative stitches, and fabric paints. Make your own Halloween stamp from a soft artist's eraser or printing block. Or adorn the bag with assorted stamps and handwritten words with an eerie theme.

Write party details on the back of the bag or on heavy paper trimmed to fit inside.

MATERIALS

For cutting and stamping:

- Mat knife; scissors; cardboard.
- Construction paper; markers.
- Artist's eraser or printing block, tracing paper, transfer paper, for making a stamp.
- Purchased rubber stamps, optional.
- Stamp pads.

For fabric collage:

- Prequilted fabric; or fabric, batting, and muslin.
- Sewing machine; or hand needle and thread.
- Shears, regular or pinking.
- Fabric scraps, fabric paints, and embellishments as desired.

CUTTING WAYS TO DECORATE AN INVITATION

Mark bag for handle 1" (2.5 cm) down from top center; mark 2½" (6.5 cm) from top and 1" (2.5 cm) in from each side; draw half circle to connect marks. Place bag over heavy cardboard; cut through both layers, using mat knife. Or cut handle, using scissors. Trace handle of first bag on remaining bags, if desired.

Mark silhouette shape on bag front. Insert firm cardboard into bag to prevent cutting bag back. Cut out shape, using mat knife. Insert construction paper backing, trimmed slightly smaller than bag; secure with glue.

Purchase Halloween stickers for quick-and-easy treat bag invitations.

HOW TO CREATE A FABRIC COLLAGE

1 Measure bag front; subtract ¾" (2 cm) from each dimension to determine fabric rectangle size. Mark rectangle on fabric, using pencil lightly. Repeat for each invitation, drawing rectangles about ½" (1.3 cm) apart. To make your own quilted fabric, sandwich batting between marked fabric and muslin; pin layers together.

2 Stitch fabric layers together along rectangle lines. Cut rectangles just outside stitching; use pinking shears, if desired. Layer a collage of fabric shapes on rectangle to make a Halloween picture. Secure shapes with craft glue or hand stitches; cover raw edges or add details, using fabric paints, if desired. Embellish with fabric trims, buttons, and hand stitches as desired. Attach collage to bag, using glue.

HOW TO CUT & USE STAMPS

1 Trace design onto paper. Transfer to smooth side of artist's eraser or printing block, using transfer paper. Cut ⅛" (3 mm) deep along design lines, using mat knife.

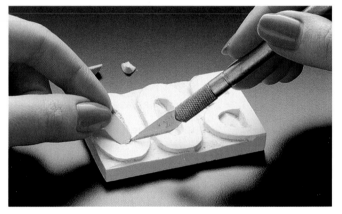

2 Remove large background area by cutting horizontally through eraser edge and up to design cuts. Cut and remove narrow spaces within design by cutting down at an angle along lines.

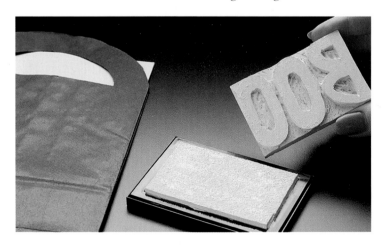

3 Insert the cardboard into bag between top layer and bottom folds and seams. Press stamp firmly onto stamp pad; lift and repeat until design is evenly coated. Press straight down onto the bag, using even pressure. Color the design, using markers, if desired.

FOAM TREAT CUPS

Let party guests create personal dinner companions when they make these easy and inexpensive foam treat cups.

Recycle assorted food cans for the cup. Consider shallow tuna cans for seated figures holding small candies. Use mandarin orange cans for short bodies or heads holding individually wrapped pieces, or use soup cans for standing figures holding stick candy and small bags.

Purchase thin sheets of colored foam to cover the cans. Cut various shapes for the bottom and back pieces; use decorative-edge scissors to cut creative details such as lace edging on a witch's petticoat or spikes on a dragon's tail, if desired. Secure the main

pieces before the party starts if the guests are young or if there are lots of other things to do.

Provide additional foam pieces and colored markers so party guests may decorate the silhouettes as they like. Layer colors by cutting desired shapes first, or trim a larger piece after it is glued to the basic shape, using the basic shape as a pattern. Use a paper punch to cut perfect holes for a ghost's eyes or to add spots to a monster. Insert small pieces into pierced foam for three-dimensional interest. Test assorted markers on foam scraps to discover how the foam color affects the marker color. Avoid handling a marked area because the ink takes longer to dry on foam than on other surfaces; it is easy to smear or transfer marker colors.

HOW TO MAKE A FOAM TREAT CUP

MATERIALS

- Small food cans, one for each cup; needlenose pliers.
- Foam sheets, assorted colors.
- Scissors with plain or decorative-edge blades.
- Craft glue.
- Clothespins; rubber bands.
- Mat knife and paper punch, optional.
- Colored markers, optional.
- Colored tissue paper, shredded paper, or plastic wrap.
- Assorted treats as desired.

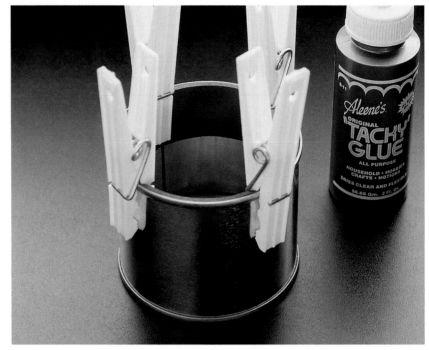

1 Compress any rough or sharp edges at upper rim of can, using pliers. Cut 1" (2.5 cm) foam strip with length equal to inner circumference of can. Secure strip to upper inner edge of can, using craft glue; place seam at back. Hold in place with clothespins until dry.

2 Place can on foam sheet; trace around the lower edge. Add design details, such as feathers, feet, or tail beyond traced circle. Cut on outermost lines. Apply glue to inner circle; adhere to bottom of can.

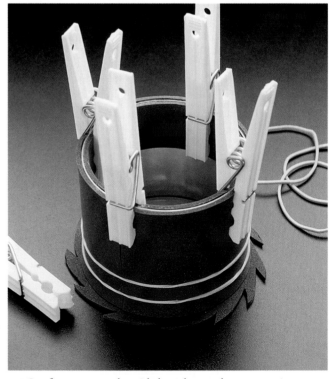

3 Cut foam rectangle with length equal to outer circumference of can and width equal to height of can. Spread craft glue evenly over foam. Secure foam to outer surface of can; place seam at back. Hold in place with clothespins and rubber bands until dry.

4 Draw silhouette pattern, using the examples shown as a guide; add height of can to lower edge of pattern. Cut out pattern and draw around it, using light pencil on dark foam colors; cut out shape.

5 Embellish silhouette as desired; attach foam detail shapes, using glue, for added dimension, or draw design lines, using markers. Cut small slits for inserting dimensional details. Apply glue to extension area of foam only; secure silhouette to back of can, over seam.

6 Add finishing details as desired. Line cup with colored tissue paper, shredded paper, or plastic wrap; fill with treats.

TIPS FOR MAKING PLACEMATS

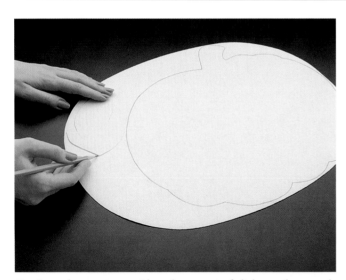

Design placemat; consider placement of dishes, silver, and napkin. Draw pattern pieces, if desired; trace around base pattern, using pencil.

Cut outer edge as desired, using regular or decorative-edge scissors or rotary cutter. Add small shapes, or cut small holes in various shapes and sizes, using paper punches.

Create colorful, sturdy placemats for your guests to enjoy, or let them create their own before sitting down to the party table.

Choose from two materials for the placemat. Cut them easily, using scissors, rotary cutters, a mat knife, or a paper punch. Add layers or decorative embellishments for a three-dimensional effect, using glue or double-sided adhesive sheets.

Purchase Kreative Kanvas® in oval placemats or large rectangular rugs. One 28" × 36" (71 × 91.5 cm) rug can be cut into four placemats. Color and define details, using markers or crayons, and apply a sealer for a water-resistant placemat.

Craft foam sheets, in a rainbow of colors, are the perfect size for rectangular placemats. Liquid spills will bead on the surface until wiped away because these mats are naturally water-resistant. Draw details carefully with markers; it is easy to smear or transfer marker colors if they are not fully dry.

MATERIALS

- Kreative Kanvas; oval placemats or rectangular rug, cut as above.
- Craft foam; 11½" × 17½" (29.3 × 44.3 cm) sheets, in desired colors.
- Scissors with plain or decorative-edge blades.
- Mat knife or rotary cutter with plain or decorative blade; cutting surface.
- Paper punches.
- Acrylic or latex paints; brushes, for Kreative Kanvas mats.
- Crayons; paper towel or newsprint; iron, for Kreative Kanvas mats.
- Sealer; synthetic-bristle paintbrush, for Kreative Kanvas mats.
- Craft glue or low-temperature glue gun, for foam mats.
- Markers, assorted colors.

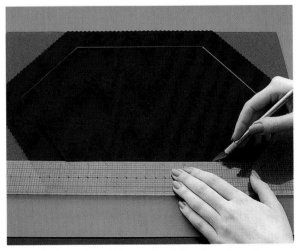

Foam placemat with contrasting border. Place two sheets together; mark border. Cut through both layers. Butt border from one sheet to center from second sheet. Glue both pieces to third foam sheet.

Color Kreative Kanvas mats, using crayons or paints and following general directions for Door Mats (page 28). Attach shapes, using glue. Outline or add details, using markers. Apply sealer to Kreative Kanvas mats, using paintbrush.

WIRED FELT PLACE CARDS

Bat wings may flap, spiders may crawl, and dragon tails may guard the candy dish when you create these felt place cards for the party table.

Use regular or decorative-edge scissors to cut felt shapes, and bend a small wire sandwiched between felt layers to give them life. Secure a wire extension at the bottom edge of creatures that sit or stand, or push it through the felt for those that fly or crawl.

Use a miniature pumpkin or a small can or box as a base for each place card. Write names directly on the felt creatures or on their bases, using markers.

HOW TO MAKE A WIRED FELT PLACE CARD

MATERIALS

- Double-sided adhesive sheet.
- Felt, assorted colors.
- Scissors with plain or decorative-edge blades.
- Paper; chenille stems, optional.
- 22-gauge or 24-gauge wire; wire cutter.
- ¼" (6 mm) dowel.
- Miniature pumpkins or small cans.
- Craft glue.
- Embellishments as desired.

1 Draw design on one side of adhesive sheet; remove paper on other side of the sheet. Adhere design to felt; cut out. Cut second felt piece to the same general shape, leaving ½" (1.3 cm) border all around.

2 Write names on selected pieces, using markers, if desired. Remove remaining paper back and lay felt on table, sticky side up. Cut wire about ³⁄₈" (1 cm) shorter than felt width; lay wire across sticky side of felt.

3 Cut wire the desired length for straight stand. Or, if curl is desired, twist wire around dowel, leaving 1" (2.5 cm) straight at end. Lap short end over shape where desired, or bend short end to 90° angle and insert through center of second felt piece.

4 Press larger felt piece to cut shape, enclosing first wire and short end of extending wire. Trim excess felt, carefully cutting around wire extension; use smaller felt shape as pattern.

5 Bend wire to shape creature as desired. Insert wire stand into pumpkin base or around stem. Or adhere to candy-filled can covered with felt. Write name on base, if desired.

DECORATIVE CANDLES

Candlescapes may be used to enhance the spooky atmosphere of any party room. There's something appropriate for every age. For safety, use long matches to light wicks that are set deep inside a candle holder, and never leave burning candles unattended.

Develop an interesting candlescape (above) with small pumpkins and gourds of various shapes, colors, and sizes. In gourds that will not tip, drill holes to accommodate small votive candles.

Children can make colorful hurricane lanterns (left) from Kreative Kanvas® and drinking glasses. The material is stiff, so even narrow extensions at the upper edge will stand. The sealer, which gives the material translucency, should be applied by an adult.

HOW TO USE SMALL GOURDS

MATERIALS

- Small gourds in assorted sizes.
- Clamp.
- Drill, spade drill bit, in size to match votive candles.
- Votive candles.

Secure gourd in the clamp. Drill candle holder hole at least 1" (2.5 cm) deep into hard-shelled gourd; use spade drill bit slightly smaller than diameter of the candle. Drill slowly, enlarging hole as necessary for tight fit.

HOW TO MAKE A HURRICANE LANTERN

MATERIALS

- Drinking glass.
- Rectangle Rug by Kreative Kanvas®.
- Scissors.
- Leather punching tool, optional.
- Markers or crayons; newsprint and iron.
- Sealer and synthetic-bristle paintbrush.
- Hot glue gun.
- Floral clay, optional.

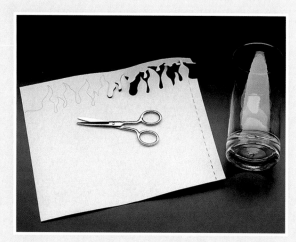

1 Measure the glass circumference and height. Add ½" (1.3 cm) to each dimension to determine the cut size of Kreative Kanvas; add more to the height if a shaped upper edge is desired. Cut shape, using scissors.

2 Cut holes, using leather punching tool, if desired. Color and seal as in steps 2 and 3 on page 29. Overlap sides ⅜" (1 cm), and secure with hot glue. Secure candle in glass with floral clay or hot glue. Drop cover over the glass.

━ MORE IDEAS FOR DECORATIVE CANDLES ━

Float shaped candles in colored water.

Paint assorted glass containers *such as stemware, glasses, globes, and vases (page 90). Pour colored sand into the containers to hold the candles and provide a background for the painted designs.*

Select a variety *of candle shapes and sizes for interest. Add press-on wax shapes for a three-dimensional effect.*

Gather a collection of witches' cauldrons *to offer a variety of warm and filling soups, stews, and brews. Arrange one in a tripod centerpiece (page 41). Paint black bowls or mugs with flames licking the sides (page 90). Reveal a favorite spell by placing an open book amid the pots; identify concoctions with hand-lettered notes, and carefully scorch the paper's edges. Select foods with unexpected color, like pistachio pudding. Or use red decorating gel on marshmallow-topped cookies. Drop dry ice in water dishes hidden behind the cauldrons for an eerie atmosphere; remember to wear gloves when handling dry ice.*

BUFFET IDEAS

Create a properly ghoulish landscape *for your guests, by building a cemetery at the buffet table. Arrange a haunted birdhouse (page 67) at the back of the table; drape the cloth over several hills and let it puddle on the floor. Add a few bare trees near the house. Scatter small monuments across the hills to name the gathered dishes; spatter-paint foam-core or precut wood dome shapes to imitate granite. Set candy worms on caramel apples and cut gelatin shapes with Halloween cookie cutters. Top a pumpkin cake with whipped-cream ghosts and sandwich-cookie tombstones. Slip silverware into napkin ghosts; cinch napkin near the center, enclosing a few cotton balls. Tuck Spanish moss here and there for effect.*

Use an interesting collection of baskets *to hold all your party fare. Purchase small hay bales at the garden center or craft store; use assorted sizes to raise some baskets above others, if desired. Drape burlap, sprinkle leaves, and nestle gourds and squash of various sizes among the baskets. Create a shelf sitter (page 75) to rule over the table. Wrap popcorn balls in colorful cellophane, and tie them with wired ribbon. Choose assorted colors of chips, and serve dip in a pumpkin-shaped bowl.*

PIÑATAS

Wendy Witch flies overhead, filled with candies for your guests. She won't share the treats unless your guests do some tricks, so invite them to break her cache with her own broom.

Use simple papier mâché techniques on a shaped paper bag to form her skirt. Wear rubber gloves and work over a plastic sheet to speed cleanup. Apply a single layer of newspaper strips to provide enough challenge for young goblins; add more layers for stronger, more exuberant guests.

Fill the piñata with small, individually wrapped candies before tying everything together with a strong nylon cord. Purchase a Nielson® topiary ball at a floral supply store for a green, dense foam head. Choose a low-temperature glue gun to secure details to the head, or the foam may melt. Select assorted black papers to make her dress, cape, hat, and boots; choose colorful papers for her hair and stockings.

Suspend Wendy from a branch, an architectural beam, or a ceiling hook. Catch all the treats on an old sheet or drop cloth for easy collecting of spilled candies when outside.

HOW TO MAKE A PIÑATA

MATERIALS

- Paper grocery bag.
- Stapler.
- White craft glue; small bowl; spoon.
- Newspaper.
- Plastic sheeting; foam brush, optional.
- Pie tin; metal washer, 1½" (3.8 cm) wide.
- Hot glue gun.
- Screw eye and small dowel.
- Nylon cord, ⅛" (3 mm).
- Nielson topiary ball, 6" (15 cm) diameter; fine sandpaper, optional.
- Styrofoam® heart, ½" × 3" (1.3 × 7.5 cm); serrated knife, for nose.
- Small wrapped candies.

- Acrylic paints.
- Crepe paper streamer, 1¾" (4.5 cm) wide, black.
- Scissors with plain or decorative-edge blades.
- Black tissue paper; ribbon, for cape.
- Tissue paper, for hair.
- Black construction paper, three pieces 12½" (31.8 cm) square; light-colored pencil, for hat.
- Glue-on eyes, 20 mm.
- Plastic spider.
- Colored paper in two colors, for legs.
- Double-sided adhesive sheets, 8½" × 11" (21.8 × 28 cm).
- Small broom.

1 Poke ½" (1.3 cm) hole through bottom center of pie tin. Press hole edges flat. Secure washer over hole, covering compressed edges, using hot glue.

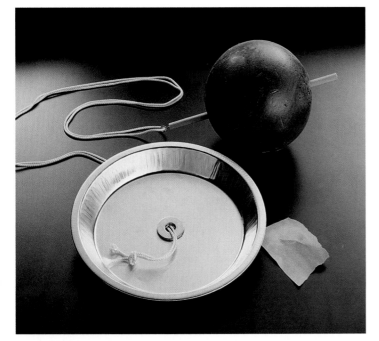

2 Sand foam ball lightly with fine sandpaper to remove ridges, if necessary; wipe with damp rag. Insert screw eye in end of dowel. Cut 3-yd. (2.75 m) length of cord; slip end through screw eye and knot ends together. Tie second knot over first; tighten knots. Insert dowel through washer, tin, and ball center. Push ball tightly against pie tin; knot cord just above ball. Remove screw eye from dowel.

3 Cut heart in half, using serrated knife. Compress hard edges of outer curve, shaping as desired. Curve cut edge slightly to fit contour of ball. Glue to ball at desired nose location.

(Continued)

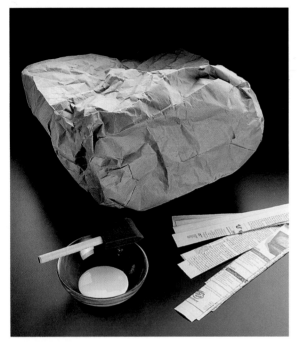

4 Crumple paper bag to soften hard edges. Push four corners in, rounding bottom; staple corner layers together on inside. Stack newspaper layers; tear 1½" (3.8 cm) strips, using straight edge, if desired. Blend ¼ cup (50 mL) glue with ¼ cup (50 mL) water in small bowl.

5 Brush diluted glue onto newspaper strip. Apply strip to bag bottom, forming small tucks in strip as necessary; use one hand to support bag from inside. Apply additional strips all around bottom of bag until lower portion is fully covered with single layer of overlapping strips. Add more layers if a hard-to-break piñata is desired. Allow bag to dry overnight.

7 Paint bag black; paint head and nose as desired. Allow to dry. Attach wiggly eyes, using hot glue. Paint mouth as desired.

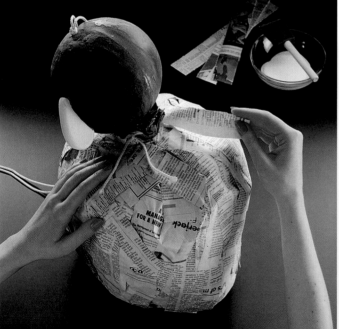

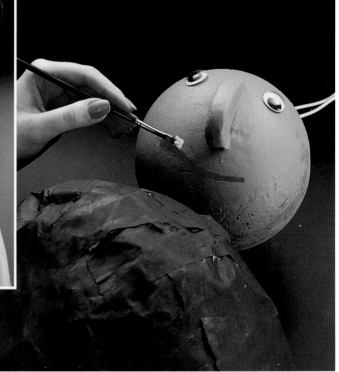

6 Fill dry bag with treats. Tuck pie tin into bag. Compress bag top; tie securely with cord, forming neck. Apply newspaper strips as in step 5, covering upper bag; lap lower strips, and extend strips as high as possible. Wrap strip around neck, covering cord. Allow to dry thoroughly.

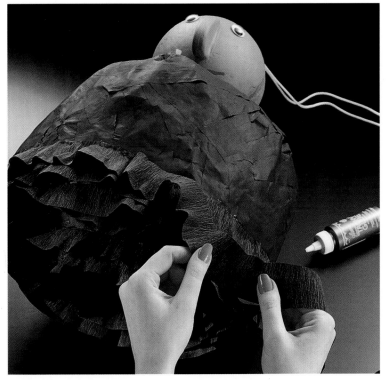

8 Stretch one edge of streamer gently to ruffle edge. Attach the straight edge to piñata body, using undiluted glue. Start at center bottom, spiraling upward; lap each layer over previous layer about 1" (2.5 cm).

9 Fuse two layers of colored paper, using double-sided adhesive sheet. Cut four strips 2" (5 cm) wide. Accordion-fold each strip; glue and lap ends to join two strips for each leg.

10 Make pattern for boot. Trace two boots on double-sided adhesive sheet. Peel off other paper and apply sheet to black paper; cut out boots. Peel off remaining paper; apply upper boot edge to lower leg edge. Apply larger paper piece to sticky side of boot. Trim excess paper; avoid cutting leg. Glue legs to piñata.

11 Fold tissue paper in half; mark two arcs 1¼" and 14" (3.2 and 35.5 cm) from fold corner. Cut on both lines through all layers, for cape; open. Tie cape around neck, using ribbon.

(Continued)

12 Cut tissue strips for hair ¾" (2 cm) wide, using decorative-edge scissors, if desired. Attach hair to head, using glue; layer long strips on back and sides to cover lower three-quarters of head. Position short strips for bangs.

13 Mark center of first hat square, using colored pencil. Measure and draw two circles around center mark; the smaller radius is 2½" (6.5 cm), the larger is 5" (12.5 cm.) Cut out both circles for brim. Cut another brim, using first as pattern.

14 Measure 11½" and 12½" (29.3 and 31.8 cm) arcs from corner of third square; cut on outer arc for hat crown. Cut from crown edge to inner arc at ½" (1.3 cm) intervals. Bend paper along inner arc for tabs.

15 Lap straight edges of crown about 2¼" (6 cm); drop one brim over peak. Glue tabs to underside of brim, using undiluted craft glue. Glue second brim to first brim, aligning edges and enclosing tabs. Slip hat over cord until it rests on head. Glue hat overlap. Attach plastic spider on hat, using hot glue. Suspend piñata as desired.

MORE IDEAS FOR PIÑATAS

Make a pink dragon piñata with a plump yellow tummy. Quarter a Styrofoam® ball for the roaring mouth and add small pom-poms for nostrils. Make horns, spikes, and teeth from colored paper.

Peter Pumpkin doesn't need a head; just a friendly smile. Cap him off with a papier mâché stem, paper leaves, and wire-core paper twist tendrils.

MUMMY HANDS

E Every mummy would love to be the life of the party! Grant that wish by letting the mummy lend you a hand or two at your next ghostly celebration.

Imitate a mummy's bandaged hand by wrapping a surgical glove, available at drugstores, with torn strips of aged batiste. Add a jeweled ring, if desired, to indicate a lifetime of wealth.

Consider a useful task that the hand may do, and shape the fingers in a way that seems to bring the mummy to life. Set the hand amid a candle-scape and place a match between two fingers. Set a hand beneath a lamp's pull chain. Or gently shape two hands around a cauldron for the buffet table.

MATERIALS

- Batiste; tea.
- Tape; 20-gauge wire; wire cutter.
- Polyester batting.
- Craft glue.
- Latex glove.
- Small unopened food can.
- Fabric stiffener.
- Match; orange felt scrap, optional.
- Glue gun and glue sticks.

HOW TO MAKE A MUMMY HAND

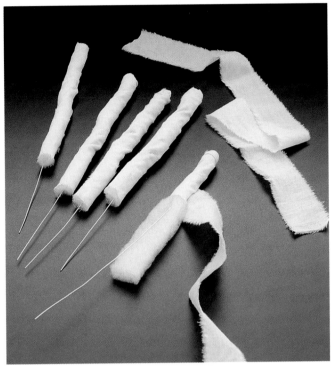

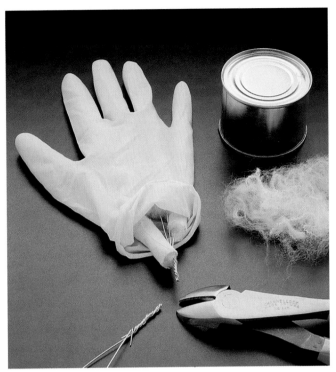

1 Tea-dye batiste; allow to dry. Tear into 1½" (3.8 cm) strips. Cut five 10" (25.5 cm) lengths of wire and five 1" × 7" (2.5 × 18 cm) strips of batting. Wrap a batting strip around each wire; secure with fabric strips and glue.

2 Insert one wrapped wire into each finger of glove; twist ends together, and trim. Insert small amount of batting to fill out palm area, if necessary. Stretch glove around can for support; tape in place.

3 Dip batiste strip into fabric stiffener. Wrap end over fingertip; turn strip, and wrap down finger. Press excess onto palm or back of hand. Continue wrapping all fingers. Wrap hand, covering entire glove and can completely. Wrap fingers and hand with several layers, for more support. Shape hand as desired; allow to dry.

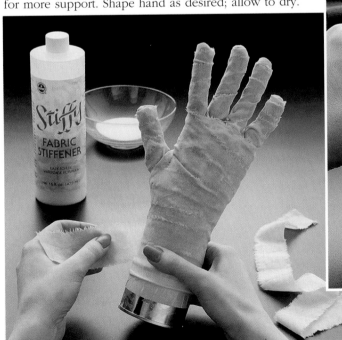

4 Wrap dry hand with layer of dry batiste strips, securing with hot glue as necessary. Leave occasional loose tail. Add any details, such as wooden match.

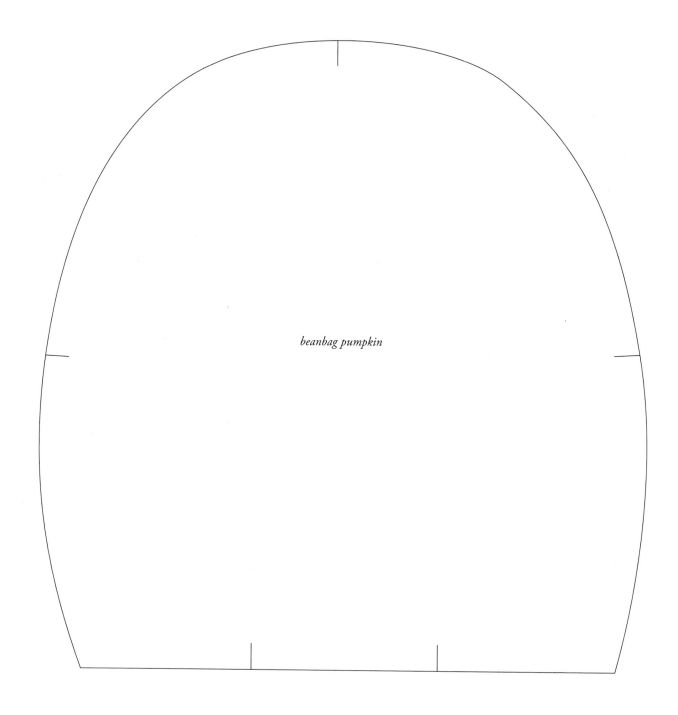

beanbag pumpkin

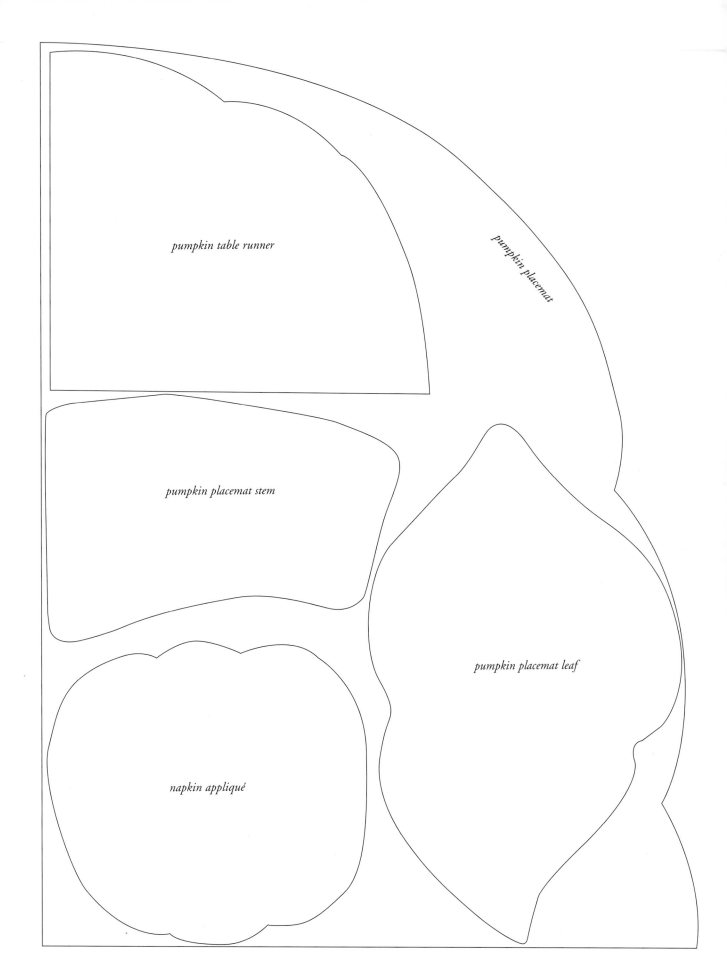

pumpkin table runner

pumpkin placemat

pumpkin placemat stem

pumpkin placemat leaf

napkin appliqué

boo frame – 1 square equals 1" (2.5 cm)

kitty frame – 1 square equals 1" (2.5 cm)

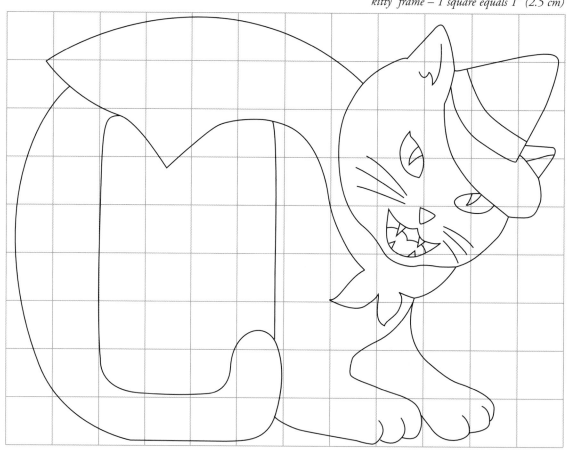

gargoyle frame – 1 square equals 1" (2.5 cm)

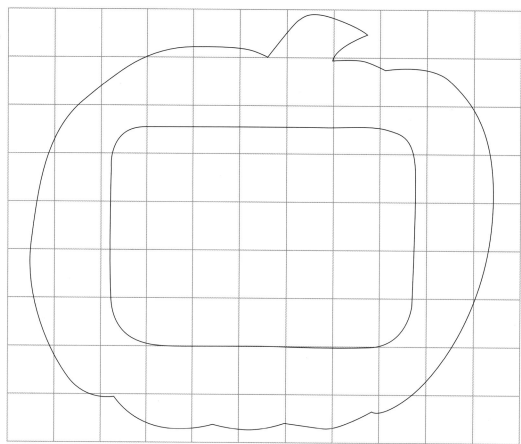

*pumpkin frame –
1 square equals 1"
(2.5 cm)*

pumpkin-carving patterns

table runner cat

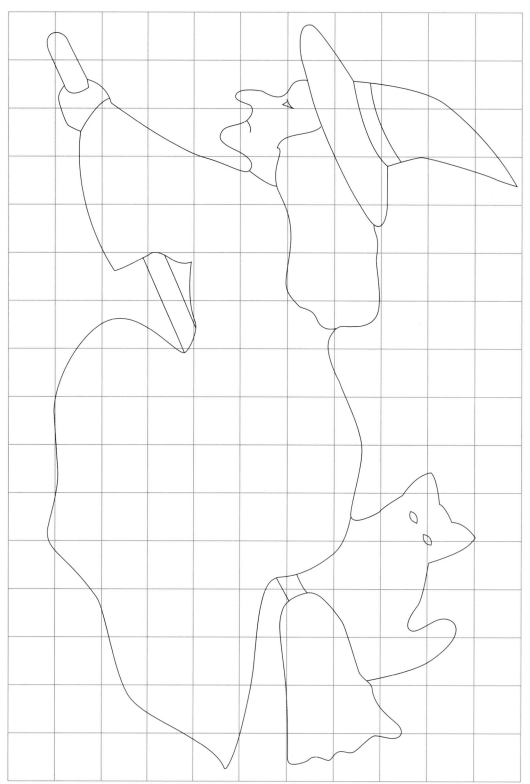

welcome witch – 1 square equals 1" (2.5 cm)

witch shelf – 1 square equals 1" (2.5 cm)

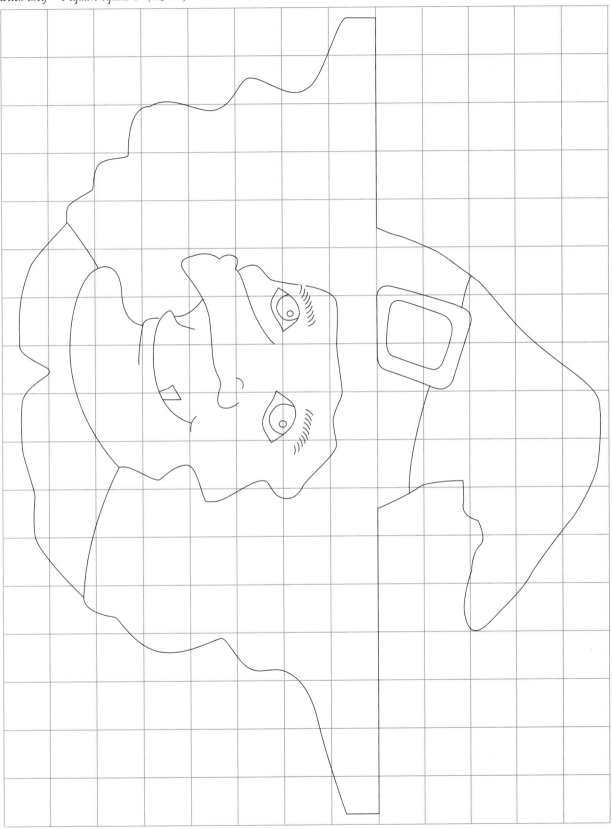

INDEX

R

W

S

T

CREATIVE
PUBLISHING
international

President: Iain Macfarlane
Group Director, Book Development:
  Zoe Graul
Creative Director: Lisa Rosenthal
Senior Managing Editor: Elaine Perry

Project Manager: Amy Friebe
Senior Editor: Linda Neubauer
Senior Art Director: Stephanie Michaud
Writer: Nancy Sundeen
Copy Editor: Janice Cauley
Researchers: Linda Neubauer, Carol Olson,
  Nancy Sundeen, Joanne Wawra,
  Caroline Weiss
Lead Project & Prop Stylist: Coralie Sathre
Project & Prop Stylists: Bobbette Destiche,
  Christine Jahns, Joanne Wawra
Sample Production Manager:
  Elizabeth Reichow
Lead Artisan: Carol Pilot
Artisans: Margaret Andolshek, Diane
  Combites, Arlene Dohrman, Sharon
  Eklund, Phyllis Galbraith, Bridget
  Haugh, Teresa Henn, Virginia Mateen,
  Christine Jahns, Andrea Jensen, Joan
  Wigginton
Senior Technical Photo Stylist: Bridget Haugh
Technical Photo Stylist: Andrea Jensen,
  Susan Jorgensen
Studio Services Manager: Marcia Chambers
Photo Services Coordinator: Carol Osterhus
Senior Photographer: Chuck Nields
Photographers: Doug Cummelin, William
  Lindner, Steve Smith
Photography Assistants: Vance Dovenbarger,
  Andrea Rugg, Tony Vavricka
Scene Shop Carpenter: Greg Wallace
Publishing Production Manager: Kim Gerber
Print Production Manager: Patt Sizer

Desktop Publishing Specialists:
  Laurie Kristensen, Jon Simpson
Production Staff: Eileen Bovard, Curt
  Ellering, Laura Hokkanen, Amy Mules,
  Brad Webster, Kay Wethern
Consultant: Dawn Anderson
Contributors: Darice, Inc.; Kunin Felt;
  Walnut Hollow

Printed on American paper by:
  R. R. Donnelley & Sons Co.
02 01 00 99 98 / 6 5 4 3 2

Creative Publishing international, Inc.
offers a variety of how-to books. For
information write:
    Creative Publishing international, Inc.
    Subscriber Books
    5900 Green Oak Drive
    Minnetonka, MN 55343

Library of Congress Cataloging-in-Publication Data

Halloween decorating.
      p. cm. -- (Arts & crafts for holiday decorating)
    Includes index.
    ISBN 0-86573-414-3 (hardcover). -- ISBN 0-86573-415-1 (softcover)
    1. Halloween decorations. I. Creative Publishing international, Inc.
II. Series.
TT900.H32H343 1998
745.594' 1--dc21   98-4402

*Due to differing conditions, materials, and skill levels, the publisher and various manufacturers
disclaim any liability for unsatisfactory results or injury due to improper use of tools, materials, or
information in this publication.*